The
Freedom
Manifesto

How to Live a Free Life in a Culture of Captivity

By Patrick Freed

Table of Contents

Introduction

When I sat down to write this book, I had one clear goal in mind, I wanted to remind my generation how to live a free life. By encouraging a culture that places zero emphasis on freedom in these modern times, we've begun to dangerously backtrack. It's been my experience that the current cultural climate has eroded the values that enabled individual freedom and replaced them with values that lead to group identity. Important, timeless principles such as responsibility, self-reliance, hard work, self-determination, spiritual connection to the world around us, polite political discourse, and the deep rooting of God in our lives have all been systematically removed from the cultural landscape.

What's left is a generation of Americans who've forgotten what it means to be free, a generation which I happen to be a part of. This book is meant to be a guide for the application of those lost principles to our modern lives, in the hopes that this generation will make better decisions that lead towards freedom and not captivity. It has been an amplification of subservience in our culture, entertainment, and news that has caused us to forget where freedom originated to begin with.

I am by no means an "arbiter of the rules" when it comes to freedom, I wrote this book just as much for my own benefit as for that of others. I too sometimes forget what it means to be free, and I have made many choices that lead to captivity in my lifetime. This book is in a sense, a culmination of the lessons I've learned up to this point in my life in relation to living freely.

I understand that the word "manifesto" has a somewhat negative connotation due to its abuse in the past. A manifesto is simply a public declaration of policy and intention, and it is my aim to help whoever's reading this book transition into a life in which they are free to pursue joy. With books such as *The Communist Manifesto* gaining new traction in our country with the younger generation, I feel it is my civic duty to put forward what I believe is a better philosophical alternative, one that has been proven to lift people out of abject poverty: freedom of thought, word, and deed.

It is my prayer that this book helps you overcome the negative aspects of your life and personality and overcome poor decision-making and political discourse so that we as Americans can all disagree peacefully again.

Chapter 1: Personal Responsibility and Self-Reliance

Responsibility is directly related to freedom. However, if there's one word that's a turn off today, it's "responsibility." Why? If you've noticed the cultural decay, defined as the erosion of morals and values in a given society, you've also noticed the distinct lack of responsibility and accountability. To define our terms, accountability refers to the condition of being answerable for the outcome of one's actions. Responsibility implies an obligation to perform certain tasks, act a certain way, or act in line with a particular set of moral codes. Responsibility directly leads to accountability, which always comes with a price. Since the price of being responsible is rather costly, most people don't want to think about how it would benefit them; that'd be too hard on their self-perception.

When I discovered my actions could directly lead me to success, I was elated! All I had to do was take ownership of myself, my life, and my actions. Once ownership had been assumed, all that was left was to stop making the same garbage decisions that had led me to my predicaments in the first place. The difficult aspects of responsibility arise from transitioning from garbage to great.

A book titled *The Power of Habit* by Charles Duhigg has quite a bit to say on this subject. On the topic of changing habits, Charles says:

> Once you know a habit exists, you have the responsibility to change it.... That, in some ways, is the point of this book. Perhaps a sleep-walking murderer can plausibly argue that he wasn't aware of his habit, and so he doesn't bear responsibility for his crime, but almost all of the other patterns that exist in most people's lives — how we eat and sleep and talk to our kids, how we unthinkingly spend our time, attention and money — those are habits that we know exist. And once you understand that habits can change, you have the freedom and the responsibility to remake them. Once you understand that habits can be rebuilt, the power of habit becomes easier to grasp and the only option left is to get to work.
> (Duhigg, 2013, p. 189)

To take control of your habits, you must understand the concept of Neural Plasticity. Neural Plasticity affects your ability to actively change your habits and be more responsible. Von Bernhardi offers a useful definition, stating:

"Neural plasticity" refers to the capacity of the nervous system to modify itself, functionally and structurally, in response to experience and injury.... Plasticity is a key component of neural development and normal functioning of the nervous system, as well as a response to the changing environment, aging, or pathological insult.
(Von Bernhardi et al, 2017, p. 1)

Habits are based on the Neural Plasticity of the brain. In other words, the more we do something, and the longer we keep doing it, the harder it is to change our behavior. But Neural Plasticity also allows us to modify our habits and our thinking as well as the literal structure of the nervous system. Through working and using the power of the mind and will, we can change our brain's thought structures and quite literally engrain in our minds how we want to live. This is the power of Neural Plasticity. The best way to apply this concept is through repetition. If you want to take advantage of Neural Plasticity, you have to be extremely consistent. To change your brain and take on new habits, you have to repeat the habits until the structure of the neurons in your brain changes completely. This is why habits and Neural Plasticity are so interlinked: when we have a habit of doing something, the structure of our brain makes it easier to maintain a habit than act contrary to it. But this also means that if we have a habit we don't like, we can change it with some effort.
If we have a habit we need to break, we must take advantage of Neural Plasticity to do so.
That being said, it can be extremely difficult to transition from one habit to the next. While your brain keeps trying to do things the same way as before, you have to make a conscious decision to go against your programming. This

7

takes a lot of willpower and discipline. But once the difficult transition period of changing the default in your brain is over and everything clicks into place, it becomes much easier to continue with the new, healthier habit.

The old saying is that it takes twenty-one days for a new habit to stick. However, in my personal experience, if you want a habit to stick for good you need to commit to three months of consistently practicing it. The first month will be difficult, especially if it's an addictive habit you're trying to change, such as smoking.

The bright side to Neural Plasticity is that once you get past the initial adjustment period, the new habit is easier to keep up. It will still take discipline and willpower for daily follow-through, but it'll also feel more and more natural as time progresses. The accountability aspect of responsibility is clear here. To reach the next stage in our lives and change our habits, we have to stay accountable to ourselves.

If we want to be responsible for ourselves we must hold ourselves accountable for our habits, our actions, and the change we hope to perpetuate through them. If we hope to be free, we must take responsibility and be accountable for our daily and long-term existence.

What does this look like? How does one take responsibility for one's own existence? It sounds rather daunting when you look at it from a bird's-eye perspective. Taking responsibility for your existence means recognizing that you are responsible for and accountable to yourself. As a certified young person, I can say with conviction and from personal experience that this is lost on many in my generation. I've seen countless examples of people giving solid advice to those they care about and never taking that advice themselves. If you want to live a free life, you must start taking your own advice. Treat yourself like a friend to be helped and taken care of, someone to be pushed in order to grow. This means you can craft yourself into the person you want to be.

If your advice is terrible, you'll learn through trial and error. Or, if you'd like to progress faster, take the advice of trusted people. Learn from them until you have enough experience to govern yourself internally.

(Of course, you still take in outside information in the process of decision-making when self-governing, but the difference lies in utilizing your internal wisdom rather than the wisdom of those just as lost as you are. An example of this is when you read a book to learn more about time management: you're still the one managing your time, but you're also taking in outside information in order to grow wiser on the subject rather than relying on suggestions from those who know nothing about it. This way you're still free to self-govern and apply what you learn, but you're also elevating your knowledge on the subject and improving your quality of life.)

Without taking responsibility for your own existence, it is impossible to take responsibility for your actions. This has led us to our current culture of captivity. A culture of captivity is a culture that purposefully pushes those in it to be irresponsible and reliant on negative habits, to ignore the natural repercussions of such behavior, and to become captive to both the negativity of their actions and those they're forced to rely on in the process.

In our culture of captivity today, we see little discussion of the ramifications of the absence of responsibility. Let's take a look at one example of the toxic lifestyles promoted by our culture that have obvious negative consequences: adult obesity.

IBISWorld, one of the largest information publishers in the world, released a report on adult obesity in 2022 that painted an eerie picture.

Over the five years to 2022, IBISWorld estimates that the obesity rate among adults aged 18 and older has increased an annualized 1.8% to 33.0 people per 100 individuals. There are a multitude of factors influencing this increase during the period, as well as over the long-term. Our modern work environment, which has become increasingly less physical, has drastically increased inactivity.
(IBISWorld, 2022)

It gets worse when we compare the percentage of obese people in America with other countries' populations. America has a total obesity rate of 36.2%. Let's compare a few other countries' obesity rates to see where we line up with the rest of the world

China: 6.2%
Russia: 23.1%
Canada: 29.4%
Mexico: 28.9%
Great Britain: 27.8%
France: 21.6%
Australia: 29%
Italy: 19.9%
Nauru: 61%
Cook Islands: 55.9%
Palau: 55.3%
Marshall Islands: 52.9%
Tuvalu: 51.6%

Niue: 50%
Tonga: 48.2%
Samoa: 47.3%
Kiribati: 46%
Micronesia: 45.8%
(World Population Review, 2020)

I could go on but you get the picture. The United States is currently the twelfth-most obese country in the world. This should be a wake-up call for everyone to start taking responsibility for themselves and take better care of themselves, but instead we've seen the opposite: a nonsensical embracing of unhealthy lifestyle habits. This seed in our culture was planted in 1969.

Originally called the "National Association to Aid Fat Americans" when it was founded in 1969, NAAFA was groundbreaking in addressing weight bias and discrimination against fat people as a civil rights issue. In their early days, they focused on letter-writing campaigns and providing a social network for its members, which included fat people as well as those who were attracted to fat people. NAAFA began holding an annual conference, which allowed fat people to meet, dance, celebrate, find community, and even find romance.
(Gerhardt, 2020)

Like most ideas, when the concept of fat acceptance was officially put into effect it had good intentions. The NAAFA wanted to help people who felt insecure feel better about themselves, and that's understandable. My problem with this is that by enabling people to continue promoting bad habits in their lives, over time the NAAFA and the fat acceptance movement created a culture of toxic behavior.

Of course, I accept every human as they are. I try to meet people where they are as a general rule. As someone who's struggled with being overweight, I can relate to how difficult it can be to live a healthy life. However, shame and guilt are natural emotions. They have their place just as joy and happiness do. When you feel shame or guilt, consider why you feel that way. It could very well be your body and mind telling you to make a change. Instead of drowning those feelings out and pretending that they aren't there, take responsibility for the way you feel, and listen to yourself.

Take your own advice. If you feel ashamed about who you are, stop doing things that make you that person. The beauty of Neural Plasticity is that you can change. If you feel shame, perhaps it could be time for a change in a different direction and to start making different decisions. Our culture today teaches us that shame and guilt are bad emotions, but no emotion is bad or good. Those are ethical labels that promote one emotion over another. Emotions have a function, just like the parts of the body. There are positive and negative emotions, but none hold moral superiority over the others. Negative emotions are there to help you course-correct. Positive emotions are there to reward you when you accomplish something meaningful. In our culture of captivity, we've been taught to abuse positive emotions to the point of overindulgence and to ignore the negative emotions telling us to make different decisions. This manifests in the obesity epidemic in this country fairly obviously.

Of course, if you have a mental health disorder because of a chemical imbalance in your brain, I'm not telling you to lean into your thoughts of self-harm or self-hatred. I'm merely stating that we as a culture have a distinct lack of responsibility when it comes to our negative qualities and emotions, opting to hide from them rather than listening to what wisdom they might have. It is only by recognizing our shame and guilt for our mistakes and wrong actions that we truly learn from them. One can't truly grasp why something was wrong without deeply feeling the moral infraction. When I was overweight, I felt depressed. I was truly sad waking up every day because I could feel the extra weight around my body and I hated it. I hated that I wasn't able to keep up with my friends. It bothered me that what I saw in the mirror didn't match the version of myself I wanted to be. Every time I did something that perpetuated the cycle of eating unhealthy food and not exercising, I got more and more depressed. More and more stuck in my ways. As I continued to not take care of myself, momentum for that lifestyle started to build.

Eventually, after being stuck in my ways for so long, it took a massive shock in my life in order for me to see things clearly. The biggest change I made was getting a gym membership and going three-to-five days a week. Starting on the path toward responsibility was difficult. I had so much momentum built up in my life from not taking care of myself that it took a lot of mental fortitude to continue down the path to responsibility and freedom.

Things got easier. It wasn't so hard to force myself to work out and eat right; in fact, I started to enjoy it. Over time, as I continued to take care of myself, my perception of myself changed. I started to like what I saw in the mirror. I didn't feel so heavy all the time. I even started to feel strong. Through taking responsibility for myself, I was starting to grasp the art of self-love.

From my experience outlined above, we can draw several principles. The first is that responsibility = freedom. By taking responsibility for my actions, I was able to free myself from my negative, unhealthy habits and the negative self-perception I had developed because of them. Once I started taking care of myself, I began to see the whole world differently.

The second principle is that you are entirely dependent on yourself for your own success. Taking responsibility for your existence means recognizing that it's all on you. You can't rely on other people to do the work for you, you have to be willing to put in the time. Your progress is entirely dependent on you. Not the collective group, not your friends, not your parents, not your partner. You.

The third principle is that momentum works both ways. This principle is called the Law of Attraction, and I'll go over it in much more detail in Chapter 2. For now, just know that if you feel like you have a lot of momentum in your life pushing you in a negative direction, all it takes in order to turn the tide is for you to assume responsibility for yourself.

Currently, according to IBISWorld, one-third of our country is overweight. That's a massive percentage. That's one in every three people. A lot of this problem stems from our culture teaching people to do what feels good in the moment rather than planning for long-term success. True personal responsibility requires that sometimes you'll have to do things that don't feel good in the moment, such as exercising, eating healthy, waking up early, staying up late studying, working hard at your job, or working off the clock on your dreams without any compensation; all of these things require responsibility and discipline.

Author, podcaster, and former navy seal Jocko Willink has a saying that I try to live by: "Discipline equals freedom." What does this mean? In order to rely on yourself, you must be disciplined and able to make yourself do things that are hard or boring and sometimes grueling and that you'd rather not do, like get up and go to work every day or take care of yourself by exercising and eating right.

There are cases in which people don't have a choice regarding their weight, for example because of a glandular problem. However, the vast majority of people who are overweight today in America just haven't taken responsibility for their own health. Staying healthy is hard, and it's black and white. Either you're healthy or you're not; there's no real middle ground. This is denied in our culture today because we've slipped into the fallacy of moral relativism.

Moral relativism is a philosophical school of thought according to which

the truth or falsity of moral judgments, or their justification, is not absolute or universal, but is relative to the traditions, convictions, or practices of a group of persons.
(Gowans, 2019)

This is a very dangerous thought to pursue, and I'll explain why. Absolute truth exists. By the logic of moral relativism, one could assert that in some cultures it's acceptable to beat your wife, and in others it's not, and that both are thus equally valid.

Except they're not. It's wrong to beat your wife. The culture that is pro-wife-beating is wrong. There are absolute moral truths that exist in this world and we as a society have forgotten that. The entire argument behind moral relativism is flawed to begin with. By the logic of the underlying principles of moral relativism, there are no concrete facts about morality in the universe, only the different cultural interpretations. However, that very statement is a concrete fact about morality. By applying the logic of moral relativism to itself, we can see that it's inherently nonsensical. Morality isn't varied. It isn't applied when it's convenient or when you feel like it. If morality exists, it always exists in every discussion. By claiming that there is no moral truth other than cultural interpretation, you are stating a moral truth and therefore creating a logical fallacy.

Not only that, but truth is freedom. Truth is defined as that which is in accordance with fact and reality. Moral relativism teaches that reality, and therefore truth, is varied rather than fixed. This implies that there is no actual truth; instead, everything is left to how individuals interpret the world around them. When there is no real truth, there is no real freedom. By teaching that there is no moral truth, no right and wrong, we allow ourselves to be led into captivity by those who wish to deceive us. Instead, we must recognize as a society that absolutes exist, and thus absolute truth exists.

"Absolute truth" is defined as inflexible reality: fixed, invariable, unalterable facts. For example, it is a fixed, invariable, unalterable fact that there are absolutely no square circles and there are absolutely no round squares.
(All About Philosophy, 2001)

To better understand this point we might look to the work of Julien Beillard (2013). In his article, Beillard takes the time to meticulously deconstruct the reasoning behind moral relativism and explain why it's a poor way to view the world. He begins by stating some truisms about what truth is. Beillard defines a true statement as something that portrays reality as it really is. That same assertion holds true for statements about morality.

Let's assume for a moment that nothing is morally wrong, despite the fact that some actions seem wrong to us. In that case, if we feel something is immoral, our assertion of its wrongness is literally false because it attributes to that thing a property that doesn't exist, like a child truly believing that Santa is responsible for presents appearing under their Christmas tree. Santa isn't actually real, and any claim that some item has the property of being made by him is factually incorrect. Those who are drawn to moral relativism may claim that Beillard's definition presupposes an "objectivist concept" of moral truth, one that relates what is said or thought about the world to the way the world truly is, independent of the different perspectives on it. In their eyes, truth doesn't involve any relation between subjective points of view and facts independent of them.

Beillard admits that he is assuming an objectivist conception of what truth is, and argues that there's no real alternative. In his words:

> Do we have any concept of truth that does not involve that kind of relation? To be sure, people sometimes say that a statement is true for one person but not another – meaning that the statement seems true to the first person but does not seem true to the second. But just as seeming gold is not a kind of gold, seeming truth is not a kind of truth.
>
> (Beillard, 2013)

Beillard goes to explain that belief and truth are not the same thing. Some children believe that Santa Clause is real and that he lives in the North Pole, when in reality he doesn't exist. Just believing in something doesn't make it morally or factually true and in accordance with reality. Similarly, if some people believe morality is relative, and this is considered false by others, this is philosophically trivial and consistent with objective moral truth. It's important to note that, interpreted in this way, moral relativism can't be supported by the mere fact of disagreement. The entire point of that argument was that moral relativism is a good explanation of moral disagreement. But again, this stems from the flaws of the human interpretation of truth, not from morality's being variable. The fact that some moral arguments are believed by some and rejected by others merely reiterates the power of perception and does nothing to detract from the necessity of objective truth outside of subjective human interpretation.

Absolute truth, or "objective truth" is the only real answer to whether mortality is inflexible or relative. Once we determine that reality and truth exist regardless of human culture's interpretation, the concept of moral relativism goes right out the window. After all, it was the leading thought in Galileo's time that the Sun rotated around the Earth. Just having an inherent belief in something doesn't make it true. Regardless of what the people at that time thought, it was still an objective fact that the Earth rotates around the Sun. I could write a book explicitly just on this subject, but I believe I've properly explained the flawed logic of moral relativism enough to properly explain my position on the subject and explain why it's inherently important to freedom.

There's a reason why I'm so passionate about this: absolute truth enables responsibility. If there's no actual truth or ethical good, everything is just relative to circumstances, meaning that morality is left explicitly in the hands of each individual culture, having no absolutes as far as what is right or wrong. Absolute truth is what allows us to say with impunity that it is morally wrong to beat your wife. Without absolute truth, we'd be unable to objectively look at the ethical problems in the world.

When a culture adopts moral relativism instead of absolute truth as its standard by which to judge ethical dilemmas, the erosion of said culture is inevitable. The people who live in those areas will become more and more sexually promiscuous as long-standing important institutions like marriage and the nuclear family begin to erode away. Just take a look at the chart below to see how badly the United States is doing in terms of the divorce rate as compared to the rest of the world:

Countries With The Highest Crude Divorce Rate

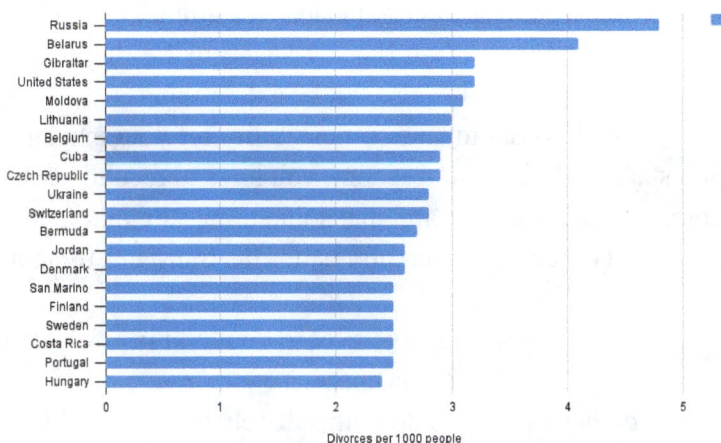

Divorces per 1000 people

(Finkbeiner and Wilkinson, 2018)

This is a chart of the twenty countries in the world with the highest divorce rate. The United States is at number four in the world for crude divorces and number six in the world for overall divorces. This is another warning sign that our culture has lost something important: a sense of responsibility to the fiber of our nation, the nuclear family. Our culture doesn't view commitments as long-term anymore, instead opting to avoid accountability for our decisions and quitting when the going gets tough.

Overarching belief systems such as moral relativism and absolute truth seep down into our daily actions in our lives. What you believe dictates a lot of what you do. By believing in something like moral relativism, you give yourself a much higher chance of allowing bad habits and toxic people into your life.

After all, if there's no moral reason not to do something other than a cultural taboo against it, the only thing stopping you from doing it is whether your individual desire outweighs the consequences for going against the cultural norms. As we'll discuss later in the chapter, individual desire can be a dark thing.

So, In order to take responsibility for your existence and start on the path to freedom, you have to recognize that there is absolute truth and that some things are inherently good, and others are inherently bad. This translates to habits as well.

Your habits also have a lot to do with the next part of this chapter.

What do habits have to do with self-reliance? Everything. What you do is who you are. I guess it could be said that you are the combination of all of your habits over time. Self-reliance is defined by the Merriam-Webster dictionary as "reliance on one's own efforts and abilities." Self-reliance lies in cultivating good habits and plucking out the pesky poor ones. Reliance on oneself is becoming more and more absent from our culture. This lack of self-reliance leads to possibly the biggest problem with identity politics and social media: when you focus solely on yourself and gaining validation of your identity from other people in order to gain social points without putting in the work to be what you claim you are, you undermine your ability to actually push yourself to grow.

If you aren't actively striving to be the version of yourself that you want or claim to be, you'll never become that person. This means that by satiating yourself with approval from those on social media or regurgitating whatever popular thought pattern exists around you at any given time, you actively commit actions that are detrimental to your growth as a person and to your own emotional, spiritual, and mental freedom.

It's my assertion that our culture has forgotten the importance of standing on your own two feet instead of leaning on others. Being self-reliant is vital to being free. Relying on others makes you captive and subservient to them. The only way to truly be free is to learn to rely on yourself for the things you need both to survive and to be happy. Self-reliance comes from a place of loving yourself enough to take care of yourself.

If being self-reliant and responsible through discipline comes from a place of positivity, it will be easier to maintain, and your internal dialogue, motivation, and the way you view yourself in general will be much kinder. In order to be reliant on yourself, you must cultivate a sense of discipline.

When you gain control and discipline in one aspect of your life, you're able to expand that out to every other part of your life. That being said, it can be difficult for a lot of people out there to stay disciplined or even to get started in taking control back. So here is the best tip to help you get started on this journey to self-reliance and personal freedom: Wake up early!

Changing habits will take time, and there will be days when you want to stay inside under the nice warm covers, pull the blanket over your face, and stay in bed. Waking up early in the morning establishes a habit and sets a precedent for you to stay disciplined for the rest of the day. Once you beat the snooze button, you've already conquered the hardest part of your day and decided that "alright, from this point on, I'm going to walk toward adversity."

Synchronicities, defined as the simultaneous occurrence of different events that appear significantly related without any connection, are a real phenomenon, and once you start to adopt the mindset of waking up first thing in the morning, you can start to apply that same discipline to other aspects of your life. It's the smallest daily decisions that over time tend to have the biggest impacts and drive real changes in your life. This is why incremental change is so powerful: it allows us to transform our lives into what we desire them to be by improving little by little every day. This is a result, again, of the neuro-plastic nature of the brain and our ability to mold it over time.

Even though we can mold our brains, we do come with some software pre-installed. Humans are naturally born with basic survival instincts. After all, the world is inherently dangerous for us and has been since our introduction into it five to seven million years ago. With everything around us having evolved to kill prey animals (which we happen to have been), it's pretty well ingrained in our brains to be on the lookout for trouble and keep an eye on our surroundings.

People today, however, are far removed from our hunter-gatherer roots. We have all of these innate instincts for survival that we ignore in favor of more "modern" approaches.

Sure, your body is telling you to eat a salad, but you drove past McDonald's and thought, "Mmmmm, that's better," so you hit the drive-through instead of going home and eating right. You don't exercise because there's no direct need to push yourself beyond what's necessary in order to get out of bed, get dressed, and get in your car to drive wherever you go (or if not to drive then to call a cab or take a train). You don't need to hunt for food or run five miles chasing your dinner. Your body is telling you, "I need exercise or I'll start to collect toxins that will cause inflammation in my muscles and joints, resulting in arthritis by the time I'm thirty." But you don't exercise because you don't have to.

We've established that the world is dangerous for humans and always has been, and that our bodies have developed natural instincts to help us overcome these adversities. It stands to reason that our minds and spirits have also developed instincts as well. Meaning that we have different lenses we can see life through in order to reach different goals. After all, perception is everything. If you're looking at life through your most high-minded lens and with the intention to do the most good, your perception of life will be of responsibility and an intense desire to rely on oneself in order to lift others up. It happens naturally.

How do we accomplish this? Well, what do you have control over? What is the one thing you can always have influence over? Yourself. You are the one constant in your life. You are always a factor in your own success and freedom; make sure it's a positive one. That's why self-reliance is so important to freedom: if you desire to live a free life, you have to make the choices that lead you toward freedom, and that means taking responsibility for the choices that lead you toward captivity. Are you keeping yourself captive in a cage of bad habits, lies, and choices devoid of responsibility and accountability?

You're captive because you're a victim of yourself and your lack of accountability for your actions. When you make poor decisions, you seldom get to pick the consequences that accompany them. How do you free yourself from your irresponsibility?

Start by fixing yourself and building yourself up. It's not selfish to work on yourself. In fact, I'd wager it's probably the most selfless thing you can do. It takes real humility to admit that you have issues, and it really takes commitment, drive, and dedication to follow through and fix those issues. It will take time to change those habits that have bound you in chains of your own unhappiness. People are fluid creatures. We constantly either progress or regress; there's no static middle ground. Make the commitment to keep getting better. If you just improve by 1% every day, you get 365% better in one year. Who would you be if you were a 365% better version of yourself? I want you to visualize what you want your life, habits, routine, career, and future to look like, and dream big; the bigger you dream, the more motivated you'll be when it comes down to the daily grind. Motivational speaker and former member of the Ohio house of representatives Les Brown has a saying:

Most people fail in life not because they aim too high and miss, but because they aim too low and hit.
(Brown, 1945)

If you have a solid view of what you want your life to look like, you can chase after it much more easily. You develop a sense of what you should be doing and what you should not continue to do, and you can begin to cut out the parts of your life that are holding you back from living freely. Not everyone can come along and not everything you do can stick around if you're going to live free. Some people are toxic. They will see your success and the happiness your freedom brings you and drag you back down to captivity out of spite. Learn to let these people go.

As far as toxic behaviors, we all have them. I've had a lifetime of toxic thought patterns, habits, and self-image. As I said before, up until about three years ago, when I decided to make a change, I was severely overweight, I was depressed, I ate my feelings, I had low testosterone levels, and all I attracted were toxic people because that's all I thought I deserved, and I had zero confidence in myself.

Suddenly, one day, I realized what I was doing. I was imprisoning myself in my own irresponsibility. I didn't deserve to have confidence because I wasn't making decisions that I could stand behind. I knew I wasn't being responsible, and I felt guilty for it. I knew what I was doing was negatively impacting my life and my own self-perception.

I was hurting my soul and hindering my own ability to fulfill my purpose and freely chase my dreams through self-hatred perpetuated by a lack of responsibility for myself. I had zero self-reliance when it came to my health in any aspect of my life. What was worse, I felt terrified of what might happen if I did become responsible, if I did grow teeth and learn to bite when I had to rather than being helpless. In my mind, it was benevolent to be helpless, a logical fallacy common to today's culture of captivity.

The integration of my shadow is what changed. Psychoanalyst and mystic Carl Jung has a saying about accepting your "shadow self" (defined as thoughts, personality traits, and emotions that are typically negative and difficult to accept):

> Your visions will become clear only when you can look into your own heart. Who looks outside, dreams; who looks inside, awakes.
> (Jung et al, 1973)

Humankind is definitely capable of horrendous and terrible acts of cruelty, and it's a very dangerous thing to assume that you're above such acts. Every human on the face of the planet is capable of doing terrible things if the circumstances and situation are correct for said acts to transpire. Human instincts are all about survival and self-preservation, making us fundamentally very selfish creatures.

> The shadow is a moral problem that challenges the whole ego-personality, for no one can become conscious of the shadow without considerable moral effort. To become conscious of it involves recognizing the dark aspects of the personality as present and real. This act is the essential condition for any kind of self-knowledge.
> (Jung and Von Franz, 1951)

The shadow is what allows us to be disagreeable, to go against the crowd, to be dangerous. However, human nature (the darker corners of it anyway) can be extremely negative. This is the negativity that comes from the low-vibrational aspects of being a living, breathing creature and having a body. Low-vibrational energy is something that we'll cover in depth in the third chapter; for now, just recognize that it's associated with the negative emotions, experiences, and darkness of life. The Holocaust in Germany, the Russian gulags, and China's bloody century, all are perfect examples of what can happen when the shadow isn't integrated.

The shadow is a subconscious part of ourselves. The overt desire to feed, reproduce, and dominate others is still strong in our minds today. Because we are further removed from the adversity of survival as we discussed earlier, the shadow can come out in social settings instead, leading to immature outbursts of the ego. The ego in this instance is defined as the part of the mind that mediates between the conscious and unconscious, allowing us to navigate and test reality.

Pretending that the less-than-desirable parts of your being don't exist will solve nothing in your quest for self-reliance and responsibility. You must accept that they are there and put habits in place in order to both integrate the shadow into your personality and keep it in check.

Taking this into account, I can reasonably assert that it is every human's responsibility to integrate their shadow. What does that mean? It means accepting the parts of yourself that make you dangerous and that are maybe not so agreeable. This doesn't mean giving in to your basest natures; it means accepting that they are there and actively striving to both keep them in check and to redirect that energy to other, more productive parts of your life.

Dangerous people change the world. Jordan Peterson once said,

The best people I know are dangerous.
(Jocko Podcast, 2019).

If you want to live a free life, you have to be willing to go against the grain, and that's a dangerous idea for the average person who's sleepwalking their way through a nine-to-five. It's a reminder that they know they're better than what they've accepted, that they've short-sold their freedom to pursue happiness in order to be comfortable.

Such people hate you out of spite for being willing to take the risks they wanted to take but never mustered the courage for. Integrating your shadow means being willing to walk alone and feel just as comfortable as you do with the group. There's a sense of empowerment in realizing you're dangerous.

Recognizing you're dangerous and integrating your shadow frees you from feeling helpless and weak. Choosing to be helpless isn't a virtue, it just means you're weak and a burden on others. Claiming weakness to be strength is a logical fallacy our culture has embraced with open arms. There is no strength, moral superiority, or virtue in being helpless. All helplessness creates is dependence on your own delusions, on those who are forced to care for you, and on your own self-doubts, forcing you to rely on the false ego rather than on your true spiritual self. (More on this in Chapter 3.)

I'm not implying that those who are physically weak due to a health condition are spiritually, mentally, or emotionally weak. Some people are even able to use their weaknesses in one category to their advantage in another, such as Stephen Hawking, who used his difficulty moving as an opportunity to expand his. My point is that making excuses and avoiding responsibility is a weakness. No one can control the circumstances that they were thrust into, but everyone can control both their reaction to and their plans to overcome their current predicament.

By taking responsibility for your existence, you empower yourself. You give yourself permission to rise above. Surely if a man who is bound in a wheelchair and who can only communicate through a computer is able to become one of the world's leading minds in the field of general relativity, you can find a way to use your circumstances to your advantage.

Keeping the integration of the shadow in mind, remember that the average person is extremely adverse to change. If you find a way to do something better and elevate your life, or to free yourself from something holding you down, hold onto that faith in yourself that things will work out. Don't listen to the naysayers who've lost sight of their dreams. Have faith in your abilities and the discipline you cultivate.

Faith will come when you've built up the discipline and put in the hours needed to hone yourself. Once you've begun to adopt the mindset of success and living free, you begin to manifest your dreams in reality. Once you have a solid foundation of work and ownership of your life, you build faith in yourself, which breeds confidence and positive energy. Focus on small wins and gradually increase them. Adopt the mindset of a winner. God didn't put you here to lose forever. If you keep persevering then eventually you will succeed, but you have to believe it will happen to qualify for that blessing.

Everyone is self-made, but only the successful will admit it.
(Earl Nightingale)

You are a product of your actions, and whether you live in captivity to yourself is dependent on you. With all of this new information, I must reiterate that being responsible for yourself and a good steward of your surroundings is a much better option than nihilistic chaos in which nobody takes responsibility for the state the world is in. Lift where you stand. If everyone lifted where they stood, the whole world would rise together.

I'd like to note before ending the chapter that, in my personal experience, responsibility and discipline have led me almost exclusively toward freedom. Loving yourself enough to stay disciplined enables you to mold yourself to your liking. Not only will taking on responsibility for your life help you grow, it will also lead you out of captivity from your poor decisions and the cage of guilt, doubt, and self-hatred imprisoning you.

Every man, woman, and child is held captive by their bad habits and poor decisions. To truly be free, you must take responsibility for yourself and make discipline a daily aspect of your life. This will give you the tools and mental toughness to break those pesky habit loops and enable you to put that energy to use elsewhere.

Taking responsibility for your own existence and learning to rely on yourself are essential habits that have been lost in our cultural climate. Philosophies such as moral relativism not only damage our ability to take responsibility for ourselves, they limit our access to freedom, preventing us from learning the skills necessary to preserve it. The best path toward freedom is one of absolute truth and personal responsibility.

Freedom comes from responsibility. Free yourself from your irresponsible habits and decisions, and watch stress, tension, and fear melt away to be replaced with a cool confidence that shatters everything. Embrace discipline. Embrace responsibility. Embrace accountability. Embrace freedom.

Chapter 2: Passion, Work, and Finance

If a man's work is his passion he will never work a
day in his life.
(Someone who's never worked)

Work is grueling by nature and always taxing in some way.
Even working for yourself, while much more rewarding than
working for other people, is still quite difficult. In my
experience, a man's work enables his passions, but turning
your passion into your work doesn't make it any less
arduous. There will always be burdensome aspects in
working toward a goal.

A much more appealing option is to use your passions
as a motivator to help you push through the difficult aspects
of work in order to accomplish goals. When you leverage
your dreams in this way, you find that the grueling features

of work are much more bearable. Not only that, it also enables a change of mentality, as you become beholden to yourself. This mental shift is the driving factor in working for yourself rather than an organization. It's unfortunate, but our culture has forgotten that passion in your own personal life and self-direction are more important than working for someone else.

The common perception that going all the way through college and getting a good payment package from a big company is getting old…. This is why the unemployment level is on the rise, even for graduates, everyone is just waiting around to be "employed," and no one is willing to create employment. This might have worked out well for Baby Boomers but it is about time that we change our thinking.
(Belyh, 2017)

Too many people today are slaves to the corporate system, selling their futures for student loans that will take ten to twenty years to pay back. All the while it's impossible to claim bankruptcy on these loans, meaning that you're stuck owing this debt for life. Without the option of bankruptcy, you become a literal slave to the system until you pay the debt off; another way to look at it is as indentured servitude.

The standard repayment plan for federal student loans is calculated on a 10-year timeline, with the expectation that borrowers should be able to pay off their debt within a decade. If that's unrealistic for someone's budget, an income-driven repayment plan might allow a qualified borrower to make smaller payments over 20 years instead.

(DeMatteo, 2020)

After you graduate from your institutional learning facility, you're thrust out into the real world, whereupon you learn that nobody cares that you have a piece of paper from a certain school that says you're an expert in whatever category you studied in. The only thing people really care about is your experience in the industry and your ability to complete a given task.

While you were studying in college for four years, becoming an "expert," you failed to gain any real-world experience of the principles you were learning, thus making you less qualified for a job than someone who has no college education but four years of practice.

Now you're stuck in this predicament, you owe tens of thousands of dollars in student loans, and you have to pay it all back somehow! So you get a job for $10–20 an hour working in a field that probably isn't the one you studied in, waiting for an opportunity to get your foot in the door in order to finally get the experience you need to be taken seriously. But what if that opportunity never comes? Meanwhile, you're stuck paying off the massive debt you owe, and sometimes the money is forcibly taken from your paycheck each week when you're already just scraping by.

Unfortunately, this is a common occurrence in the United States, as people trade their financial independence and freedom for a worthless education. As a certified young person, I can say with impunity that my generation was lied to. The story we were all told throughout our formative education was that if you graduated from college and got good grades throughout, these big companies would be chomping at the bit to have you work for them. This may be true to a certain extent—formalized education definitely has its place in certain fields like medicine and engineering (I've looked into it and I've struggled to find any way to learn open-heart surgery entirely without a college degree)—but as far as the corporate world goes, it is much cheaper to hire people for positions internally and to train them to do the job rather than taking on someone who is educated in the field but not in the particulars of your company. College graduates are looking for jobs that pay enough to make a dent in their student loans and may be expecting a higher salary than someone you already employ.

If you're an employer you'll save money in the long run by promoting the employees you already have (who will be thankful for even a small raise) rather than hiring from outside the company. The person who works for you is already familiar with how the company operates, so you'll save a lot of time training them. On top of this, you know their track record, so there's much less of a risk. People are always happy when you give them a raise; it doesn't matter if it comes with some extra work attached to it because most people only see the small victories. Someone lower in the company hierarchy will fill the now vacant position, all the way down the ladder until there's a gap that can't be filled from the bottom. That's where you enter the workforce: the bottom.

This means that, yes, it's entirely possible to make a solid career out of some positions that don't require specialized training, and all without a college degree. It's more work and requires investing time in yourself, but it's entirely possible, especially after the internet boom. This is a far cry from the story we were told in the public education system. The fact of the matter is, that we live in a meritocracy. A meritocracy is

a system, organization, or society in which people are chosen and moved into positions of success, power, and influence on the basis of their demonstrated abilities and merit.
(Merriam-Webster)

Upon learning this new information about how the job market actually works in the corporate world, young people tend to change their approach from an education-based model to one based on experience. Even if they decide to get a formal education, their new top priority is to show how they're useful to a future employer rather than simply to get a degree, or they change their goals, aiming to become employers rather than just being employed. After all, just getting a degree in a field of study doesn't entitle you to a job in that field, and it certainly doesn't prove your competence in that area. Getting a college education is all well and good, but without practical experience actively applying what you are learning to the real world, it doesn't amount to much as far as functionality goes.

I'm not saying a college degree is useless, but I *am* saying that as a culture we are veering too much away from college alternatives and producing quite a few overeducated idiots.

There are a *lot* of options out there if you're looking to get an education without paying through the nose for it, from internships to apprenticeship programs, self-led courses, accredited certificates, studying on your own and passing accredited testing requirements; these are all options for those who desire to circumvent these college institutions and the massive debt they create.

Obviously this is a lot more work than taking the path well-trodden and getting student loans to attend these universities. If you have the mindset to work for yourself rather than for other people or institutions, however, you will see it as a necessary step on your journey towards self-reliance.

My father has a saying that he'd repeat to me very frequently growing up: "Everyone has chains, but in America you get to pick the color of the chains you wear." This meant that everyone is a slave to the system but we have the freedom to choose how we serve it. In my opinion, the shackles of self-employment are vastly easier to carry and a lot more stylish than the chains of massive college debt.

The shift in mindset from working for others to working for yourself needs to take place on a mass scale. Too many people are too invested in the idea that "if I give this organization my best years and put everything I have into them, I'll be taken care of." You won't be. These giant corporations don't care about you. Make the mental shift to seeing yourself as your boss. You may not be self-employed, but you work for yourself every day regardless of whether you own a company. Your time is yours; start investing it in yourself rather than in pointless, time-wasting tasks like watching tv and playing video games in order to better your situation. If you're willing to bust your ass every day working for someone you don't even like just to survive, why won't you put the same amount of effort into yourself?

Put in the time to cultivate a real skill, something that you can market and actually become proficient at. A skill that is useful to the world around you. Even Jesus was a carpenter. No matter what you want to do with your life, find something you're good at and cultivate it into a skill that can make you useful and appealing to those you want to help.

Because we live in a meritocracy, once you have a skill cultivated and well defined, news of your talent will spread by word of mouth. Soon you'll get to pick your customers, and not the other way around. Even better, because of the internet, learning has become basically free. Anyone can hop on the web and look for tutorials or how-tos on getting started for virtually anything.

This calls the necessity of these giant brick-and-mortar colleges into question. If people can learn on their own or through a mentorship program, why is college still pushed so heavily on young people today?

Because colleges teach subservience. They reinforce the teachings kids receive up through high school to do as they are told, to listen to authority figures, and to avoid thinking for themselves. This underlying process of shaping the minds of young people involves the systematic removal of their desire to be free through social conditioning. If a college can indoctrinate you in a certain ideology (I'm referring to the increase of Marxist and communistic ideologies actively being taught on college campuses), make you a slave to the system with debt you may never be able to pay back, and send you off to work for a corporation for much less than you desire, it sounds like an extremely good situation for those in power but an unfortunate one for you.

The solution to this is to remember that you are free to learn outside of these mega-college organizations. We live in a time when colleges are starting to become obsolete. If you can become good at something without needing a college education, you circumvent the necessity of going into debt in the first place. If you do need formalized education for your field of study, seek out an apprenticeship or mentor program. There are valid alternatives to most college institutions.

Or you may choose the entrepreneurial option, as I did. Throwing yourself to the wolves and starting your own company is very difficult, and I respect anyone who can successfully run a company at a profit, no matter how little the profit may be. No matter what path you choose to take, true financial freedom lies in not relying on others for your own income and eventually only relying on the systems you put in place to make you money autonomously instead of trading your time for money. The secret is to build streams of passive income. Passive income is money earned without your being actively involved in the process.

Passive income is a good sign of financial freedom. Being able to live off of systems autonomously bringing in profit while you go do other things with your time is extremely freeing. My father had another saying he'd tell me all the time growing up: "When you're truly rich, you have both time and money, and when you're truly poor, you have neither."

Your financial freedom isn't dependent on whether you have a lot of money. The mark of true financial freedom is having income without trading your time for it. This is accomplished through asset and business ownership. That's the reason so many people dream of starting a company and buying real estate. If you can put all of the systems in place and slowly grow them, after a while you'll be truly taken care of. After all, when you work for someone else, you trade your time for a limited amount of money. When you work for yourself, you choose when you trade your time, and the ceiling for potential earnings is unlimited. Not to mention you can lose your job as an employee at any time. But unless something bad happens to your company, you can't be fired when you're self-employed. Even though it's more unpredictable than being an employee, it's still the better option. This is because over time you will cultivate a set of skills that help you thrive in that environment, making it a more stable option than working for someone else.

The hard reality is that life is unpredictable and unstable. There is a difference, however, between losing your job and losing your company. I have lost both at different times in my life. Both are difficult. The difference lies in how much you learn and the person you become. If you lose a company, you've learned more, refined yourself to a much higher degree, and gained an understanding of how to become self-sufficient outside the system. Whereas if you lose a job, you're cast into a sea of doubt, entirely unsure of what to do or even if you can survive without paychecks from a corporation. When you own and run a business, you learn a skill set just like any other job. That skill set and the principles you learn from doing the work are retained over time. If you ran a company once and it got so far, you can do it again with something else, apply what you learned the first time around, and go further.

Job security isn't a real thing. It's a myth. A well-played con on the American people. When you're employed with a company, most of the time it's "at-will employment," meaning that you can leave anytime and the company can fire you at any time without legal liability. This is a good thing if you believe in meritocracy. If you're good at your job and you do it extremely well, your job is more or less secure. If you're bad at your job you'll be slowly replaced with someone who is more competent. However, even if you're incredible at your job, the company may downsize and need to cut staff. Or perhaps, for whatever reason, you may make a strange, out-of-place mistake that ends up costing them thousands of dollars. Poof. Your job is gone. All that time and energy you've invested into working for them is suddenly nothing. Sure, you learned a skill, but to find a similar job with a competitor you may very well have to climb the corporate ladder again, and nothing is guaranteed.

At least when you have to close down a failed company, you take with you the skills you learned, connections with all of the people you were doing business with in the area, a reputation for being independent, and if you were smart, a list of potential customers and their contact info for marketing when you're ready to get the word out on your next project; not to mention the experience of putting everything together the first time, so that the second time around will be far easier.

The sad reality is that the relationship between employee and employer is purely a business one. In smaller companies you can argue that you're "friends" with your boss. But they still sign your paychecks every week or two, and while they hold that power over you there will always be a difference in your hierarchical standing. The only way to make sure you are truly taken care of is to start getting into the business of working for and investing in yourself.

This doesn't have to mean starting a company, it could be something like learning a language or a new skill, but you have to start seeing yourself as the person you're beholden to. Working for yourself in the pursuit of happiness is the path toward freedom. If you're selling your time every day to a corporation, you are depriving yourself of the work you could be putting into yourself. All that time and energy spent working for other people could just as easily be put into your own life; the amount of work would be relatively similar and you'd get to see in real time how far you've progressed.

If you desire to be free, you must be willing to put in the work necessary to live a free life. Freedom takes maintenance, and without the willingness to put in the work to maintain a free lifestyle, over time it will disappear. A willingness to work has been a mark of success throughout history. Life tends to reward those who are willing to put in the time in the right places. The key phrase here is "right places." Those who put in the hours working toward goals that are not worthwhile will have wasted both time and effort. What better goal is there than to pursue bettering yourself in service of your fellow man? Everyone has a dream they want to strive for; push yourself to become the version of yourself that can live that dream.

Use your passions as a motivator for you to overcome the difficult aspects of your career. The more you progress financially, the better equipped you will be to follow your dreams. Money doesn't buy happiness, but it can buy things that enable you to have a better quality of life, which alleviates quite a bit of stress and makes the pursuit of happiness a hell of lot easier. There are no problems as uniquely uncomfortable as money problems. Few things make you feel quite as trapped as debt or financial burdens.

On the topic of debt, I would say to avoid it at all costs unless you know how to play the game. Compound interest is a scary thing that many in this world have fallen victim to. If you are in debt, stay up to date on your payments! This is crucial. Don't pay the minimum amount; that will only pay off the interest on the money you owe.

Instead, put as much money as you can afford towards paying it off, as that's typically the best deal in the long term. Ideally, you want to only go into debt when you know you will be able to pay it back, and if you do take on debt, get out as fast as possible.

The reason that this is so important is because of how the rich see money. The thing that so many people don't get about money is that it's not a static object. Money is magnetic and fluid: the more you have, the more you attract. If you're in debt, you are attracting more debt. On top of that, it damages your self-image, which leads to a lack of confidence, which in turn perpetuates a cycle of negativity. This is actually just the application of a general principle called the law of attraction A book titled *The Secret*, written by Rhonda Byrne, defines the law of attraction as follows:

Basically, The Law of Attraction tells us that whatever we believe, we will manifest.
(Byrne, 2016)

The reason the law of attraction is so powerful in relation to financial matters in general is rather obvious, but I will make a point to state it specifically. If you're in debt and constantly aware of it, the probability of your manifesting more debt in your life is high; this is because it's already happened before and you believe it could happen again, and therefore it may.

The solution: change your mindset. The power of perception is a real phenomenon. Financial success, in my experience, is just as much about mindset, manifestation, and abundance as it is about numbers and experience.

The law of attraction applies to every aspect of your life. It applies in negative ways as well. If you concentrate on a bad situation and put energy into negative possibilities, they will eventually come true. If you want to reach your dreams, you must believe they will happen for you and put in the work in order for them to manifest. You have to believe that you are capable of changing your situation. Listen to your internal compass telling you your next move, believe in yourself, and strive for it.

If you plan on being financially successful, you'd better stop doing what everyone around you is doing. You are the sum of the five people you spend the most time around: this is refers to the law of averages, meaning that if you spend your time with a particular group of people, you will become the average of that group. If the people you hang around with are disciplined, successful, and financially literate, chances are those qualities will rub off on you and increase your chances of having those positive aspects in your life. However, if they aren't financially literate, disciplined, and successful, they could be preventing you from unlocking your full potential. Not only that but the things people around you manifest also affect you, so it's incredibly important to choose your friends carefully and to be private with your finances as well. Share those important details with only people that you trust.

How does freedom tie into this? If you can change your mindset, financial freedom is a real possibility. A lifestyle whereby you work for yourself rather than being held hostage by a paycheck is immensely freeing. Having complete control over your schedule and the freedom to travel and choose where and when you'd like to work: all these things come along with working for yourself rather than a company. The peace of mind you feel waking up every morning knowing that the hard work you're going to put in that day will be for your benefit and not your employer's is a boost of serotonin like no other.

Whatever your life's work is, do it well. A man should do his job so well that the living, the dead, and the unborn could do it no better.
(Martin Luther King Jr)

Our culture today has deemed failure a negative thing. Failure can be the best thing to ever happen to you. Failure is humbling, it reminds you that you have more to learn. I'm glad the Wright brothers failed all the times they did while making the airplane, because eventually, when they made one that worked, they *knew* it worked. If you can find within yourself the tenacity to get back up after every failure, eventually you will learn how to stop failing as frequently. It's human nature. When applying this to self-employment and the financial aspects of life, you must be willing to work hard enough to fail your way to success. If you work for yourself, you only truly fail when you give up on becoming the person you want to be.

You will attract wealth in whatever you do as long as you believe it's going to happen. In order for you to believe it will happen, you must put in the work to cultivate faith in yourself.

I have a saying: "Do the f*ck out of everything." It's what I nonchalantly term my best weapon. Working hard, going the extra mile, staying late, and doing what others aren't willing to do, that's the secret to succeeding financially. In order to unlock the belief in yourself that lies within you, you *must* set a consistent pattern of completing what you start, and everything you do must be done with a sense of excellence and thoroughness. Eventually, through daily practice and perseverance, excellence will become effortless. The neuroplastic aspect of your brain that we discussed in Chapter One dictates that once we have a habit in place, it becomes drastically easier to maintain. In terms of financial excellence, establishing a pattern of consistent responsibility and discipline will pay massive dividends in the long run.

Create a budget and stick to it! This is so incredibly important. The best way to live below your means and save money each month is to create a list of your expenses, including the expenses you tend to ignore, such as eating out or drinking at a bar; everything must be accounted for. Once the expenses have been written down, calculate how much on average you make each month. The amount of money you make each month must be more than you spend each month in order to stay in the black. If you spend more than you make, you're on the fast track to financial ruin.

Another good way to stay ahead of your finances is to reconcile your accounts each month to confirm that your account balance matches your statement from the bank. If something seems fishy or numbers seem off, there's a good chance you misplaced some cash or forgot about an expense. Your budget will change over time; take these monthly reconciliations into account when revising your budget. Eventually, managing your finances will become so easy you'll scarcely have to think about it.

On the subject of finance, I'd like to recommend a book that was recommended to me by a mentor of mine. This book changed the way I execute every task in my life. It's titled *The 4 Disciplines of Execution* and was written by Chris McChesney, Sean Covey, and Jim Huling. In this book, the authors dive headfirst into how to create lasting change in your business and life by dedicating 80% of your time to your "whirlwind" and the other 20% of your time to short- and long-term goals. This allows you to make sure you're keeping up with the daily maintenance of your life or business while putting that 20% toward new goals and cultivating habits to reach those goals. It's an amazing time-management trick that has saved my hide more than once. In case you're unfamiliar with the concept of the whirlwind, it refers to those things that must be done in both business and life: cleaning your home, grocery shopping, budgeting, exercising, working your day job, and so forth. The whirlwind is best described as the daily maintenance of your life. If you manage a business, tasks such as generating new leads, reconciling accounts, marketing, advertising, and hiring new staff are all examples of the whirlwind in a business context. The whirlwind must be kept up with or you'll be swept away by it. But it can't take up all of your time or you'll never have the opportunities to learn new things or make lasting changes in your life/business. By dedicating 80% of your time to the whirlwind, you allow yourself to keep up with the maintenance of life while still leaving the other 20% to pursue new projects.

The 80:20 rule applies to many aspects of life. For instance, it is said that 20% of your work and how you spend your time should make up 80% of your income. Unfortunately, the 80:20 rule goes both ways, and many people give up 80% of their time in order to make a living wage. This is called active income, otherwise known as the trading of time for money. Again, these people are almost exclusively employees who work for someone else.

It is my personal experience that working for other people kills the creative entrepreneur in your soul and teaches subservience. It's impossible to be completely independent and free and have someone else signing your paychecks. The good news is that the 80:20 rule can help you get out of working for other people and get you into business for yourself. It's the same principle as the whirlwind. Simply keep putting 80% of your time into your job, and put the other 20% into your new business venture.

When I started my first company, I was working two jobs and was fed up with the sixty-hour weeks. I was twenty years old and I was done with working for other people. I saw the way some of my previous and then current employers ran their companies, and the longer I paid attention, the more I understood how they operated.

If we define a business as a vehicle for bringing in wealth using a set of systems, then in principle, every business has a similar structure regardless of what they do. I began to read books about business management and asked my bosses questions about how certain things were done and their reasoning behind doing them that way. I wanted to understand the systems of the businesses I was already familiar with before creating my own.

After I was familiar enough with the systems of the businesses I worked at, I put the 80:20 rule and the law of attraction into effect by giving notice at one of the jobs I held. The other job I had provided just enough income to ensure my bills were paid. Now I've freed up about 20% of my day to build the business while dedicating the other 80% to my day job. Luckily I'd been working two jobs for the previous two years, so working on the business and working full time wasn't too different from what I was used to. Eventually, I got to the point where I was so busy with the business that my day job was interfering with its growth. This was the critical jumping-off point for me. Thankfully, my mentor was there to give me the extra push I needed to hand in my notice to my final remaining day job. Now I was completely free to work on my business full time.

The reason I'm telling you this story is to emphasize the power of the 80:20 rule. If you are consistent about how you use your time, particularly when it comes to finances and running a business, you will see great results, especially when the 80:20 rule is used in conjunction with the law of attraction.

Now, how does passion play into all of this? Passion should be the gasoline on the fire that pushes you to succeed. If you're passionate about success and self-improvement, you'll always be pushing yourself to be better and to stay ahead of the curve. The work you do, although grueling at times, is necessary for your passions (that is, your dreams) to take form. The dream is where the passion lies. Keep your dream in the front of your mind as much as possible. Not only will it motivate you, it will have a huge positive impact on your decision-making. You need that daily reminder of your goals, dreams, and purpose in order to stay focused on the work ahead, to push through the rejections, to shrug off the betrayals. These things are going to happen to you. As Les Brown once said:

It's called life. Eighty percent of people don't care, the other twenty percent are glad it's you!
(Brown, 2021)
I like to remember a principle called Murphy's Law: anything bad that *can* happen probably *will* at some point. What does that mean for you? Toughen yourself up, because you're going to have to be resilient if you're going to reach your passions and dreams!

Life is painful regardless of whether you're trying or not; negative things happen every day to millions of people who've already given up. The hardships don't stop if you give up your passions and dreams and just decide to have no purpose. Hard times are coming whether you've got a dream or not, so find something worth weathering them for. Find a dream, a passion, a goal, something to strive toward, and throw yourself into it to make yourself stronger!

Jordan Peterson talks quite a bit about the circuitry in your brain in his lectures online. In his video "Biblical Series number XI: Sodom and Gomorrah" he explains in great detail why it's imperative to walk towards the adversity you face in life rather than allowing it to come to you. Dr. Peterson makes the assertion that the clinical data on the subject of facing your fears is incredibly clear. When you're trying to help people who are afraid, possibly depressed, and definitely anxious, you have them lay out what they're anxious about and why they're afraid in great detail. After they've properly explained why they're anxious and what they're afraid of, you break that fear up into smaller, hypothetically manageable problems, and have that person expose themselves voluntarily to the thing they're afraid of. Through that process, in Dr. Petersons words:

> What happens is they don't get less afraid, that isn't what the clinical literature indicates exactly. What happens instead is that they get braver. And that's not the same thing right? Because if you get less afraid it's like, "well the world isn't as dangerous as I thought it was. Silly me." If you get braver that's not what happens. What happens is you go "Yeah the damn world is just as dangerous as I thought, or maybe it's even more dangerous than I thought, but it turns out there's something in me that responds to taking that on as a voluntary challenge, and grows and thrives as a consequence."
>
> (Peterson, 2017)

Jordan Peterson goes on to explain the clinical data more in depth. He asserts that there is no doubt about this in the psychophysiological findings. It's quite clear from those studies that if you impose a stressor on two groups of people, and have one group voluntarily pick up the challenge, and the other group have the stressor forced onto them, those who voluntarily took on the stressor utilize an entire different psychophysiological system to deal with it. When someone voluntarily takes on adversity, they use the system that's associated with approach and challenge, not the system associated with defensive aggression. The system associated with challenge is also considered to be associated with positive emotion, and much more manageable than the system associated with defensive aggression, which is also associated with our prey animal instincts.

The part of your brain that you use when you operate out of fear is different from the part you use when you rise to the occasion and meet challenges head-on.

When you voluntarily accept difficulties, you open up your mind to your creative genius and are able to come up with real solutions to fix the problems. Ideally, you should be seeking out responsibilities and challenges so you can grow, work on your dreams, and help the world in the process. One of my favorite quotes from Dr. Peterson is:

You want to take on responsibility. You want to take on the heaviest load that you can conceive of that you might be able to move because it gives your life nobility and purpose. And that offsets the tragedy.
(Anderson, 2018)

Passion, love, dreams, and goals, all offset tragedy. The tragedy of life is coming either way; if you're actively pushing yourself to pursue your passions and dreams, to become better and put love into the world, you will be better off when it does eventually strike. Use your passions as fuel for your work and career and the financial wealth that we all seek will come naturally.

All of the concepts in this book are connected. When you free yourself from one bad aspect of your life, it weakens the bonds the other negative parts have with you. It shows you your real, raw power over your life. Once you change the default setting in your brain from "I'm a lazy loser" to "I'm a hard-working winner," those bad aspects don't hold you nearly as much, because you're actively fighting back to get the life you want. This changes your perception of yourself. It's a lot harder to see yourself as a loser when you're the hardest-working guy in the room. If you want to have financial freedom with both time and money at your disposal, you have to be willing to work harder than everyone else around you.

Grant Cardone, whether you love him or hate him, has quite a bit to say about outworking others. Grant has run several successful enterprises, and in his book *The 10x Rule* he outlines a way to be successful by amplifying your vision.

To be successful, you need 10X more effort and commitment than the average person.
(Cardone, 2011)

The 10x rule, put simply, requires being willing to push yourself ten times harder than everyone else, setting goals that are ten times bigger than you think you can muster, and asking for ten times more than what you think you need. This mass multiplication of effort rockets you toward success and helps you minimize the aspects of your life that are holding you back.

When you ask for ten times what you think you need, even if you don't get all of what you ask for, you get much more leeway in terms of what you have to work with. It also changes others' perception of your value: it says to them that you see yourself as worth that much. This enables you to drastically improve your circumstances. When you also apply yourself and work ten times harder with ten times the focus on your dreams and passions, the results are undeniable. This is the power of focus and consistently pushing yourself to be the best version of yourself through hard work and perseverance.

It's difficult to put the 10x rule into effect. At times you'll want to go the easy way. You'll have to stay in and focus on your dreams instead of going out. You'll have to sacrifice relationships with people who don't support you. Your focus has to be on self-improvement and goal fulfillment. It is too easy today to be distracted by everything around us. From our phones, to TV programs. Even to other people, we are constantly surrounded by distractions every day. It is our job to cut out the noise and distractions preventing us from reaching our purpose in our lives.

If you're competing with someone just as competent and experienced as you are, the only way to win against them is through strategy and hard work. You must hone yourself to become not only dangerous, as we discussed in Chapter One, but also efficient, dedicated, and driven. There are a lot of people in the world; I promise you that some of them want the same thing you do, and they're just as skilled as you are. The only way to compete against such opposition is to work harder and have a better strategy than them. In order to be financially successful, you have to take strategy into account. Simply working hard without a clear view of what you want the next step to be will result in you spinning your wheels and going nowhere. In order to develop a solid strategy for financial success, you must always be working on yourself in order to improve and keep ahead of the curve.

You can't stop working on yourself. You are never done. The secret to learning is that the more you learn, the more you realize how much you don't know. The further you progress toward self-betterment, the more you will see how much you have to improve. The further you progress toward freeing yourself from your negative habits regarding work, finance, and passion, the more you will find not only success but a fulfillment like none other. To be financially free, no more a slave to the corporate system, stop trading your time for money and instead take both and invest them into your success. All of your hard work will culminate in the form of a lifestyle of freedom like no other. To work for yourself in pursuit of your own happiness and success is a manifestation of freedom. When you free yourself from the toxicity around finance in our culture today, a rich fulfilling life is just around the corner. Embrace working for yourself. Embrace your dreams. Embrace freedom.

Chapter 3: Spirituality, Ethics, and Morals

The universality of spirituality extends across creed and culture. At the same time, spirituality is very much personal and unique to each person. It is a sacred realm of human experience.
(Verghese, 2008)

It is my belief that ethics and morality are explicitly missing from today's culture and social climate because of a shift away from spirituality, and towards a reliance on pleasure for individual fulfilment rather than relying on the spirit.

Spirituality and connection to your inner spirit are vital to living a free life, one in which you relate to the world around you on a spiritual level. Throughout this chapter, I will dive deep into the reasons why being connected to your inner spirit is imperative for living a free life.

As I'm twenty one, I grew up around the moral decay, propaganda seen on tv, the internet, the school system, the decline of our government, and the moral destruction of our society. The spiritual decline of our culture has been evident for quite some time. The pushing of pornography, the removal of discussions about God from our schools (I am not referring to the indoctrination of children into a religion, but only saying that we should educate children about different belief structures and allow them to choose what resonates with them), and the increased focus on the ego in pop culture have eroded the connection many feel to their spiritual selves. These are just a few of the many ways our culture has taken stances against spirituality.

I've noticed a very disturbing shift these last two years, however. Since 2020, when the world shut down and everyone interacted with each other only on social media, we've become disconnected spiritually from each other at a far greater level than before. In 2020, between the election and government-enforced lockdowns, we saw an amplification of the spiritual disconnectedness of our culture.

There's a different mechanism in your brain that you use when you interact with someone face to face as opposed to through a digital screen, and you miss all of the verbal and social cues when communication takes place over text. This is why often people are much more polite in person. However, since the lockdowns, quarantining, and enforced mask wearing, during which time people's feelings of disconnectedness were amplified by polarizing politics, people have begun to treat others in person the same way they treat them online.

A lot of this has to do with the political tribalism of our time (more on this in chapter five), but a fair amount is due to a lack of basic ethics and morality in our culture.

Though often seen as one and the same, ethics refer to the code of conduct that people live by, and morals refer to the personal values of each individual person. In our spiritually dead culture, we praise criminal behavior and the sexualization of young women in music. We glorify drug use and substance abuse rather than healthy lifestyles. We praise the ego and ignore the spirit.

Our culture has been so far removed from reality that we enable these unhealthy lifestyle choices by way of group encouragement and are subsequently baffled when these poor decisions have negative consequences. As discussed in Chapter One in connection with the obesity epidemic in America, our culture has been praising unhealthy decisions for so long that our perception of health has become entirely warped. This has a direct negative effect on your spiritual health and the connection you feel with your spirit.

We've completely removed the spiritual aspect of everyday life from our society. That's a big problem because human beings are inherently spiritual creatures experiencing a human life. This makes your spirit the most important part of who you are.

It's the removal of this spirituality that has caused the moral and ethical decay of America. It is by nourishing our spirits and cultivating a connection with them that we are truly fulfilled in this life. The spirit is your moral compass in a sense: listening to it, following its lead, and amplifying it is how we as humans achieve true joy in life. Without it, people feel hollow and empty, like there's a hole inside of them, eventually developing a sense that something is missing. To cope with this gaping hole in their lives, people cling to belief structures that deny this fundamental part of themselves, namely nihilism and atheism. Nihilism is the complete rejection of moral principles due to the underlying belief that life has no inherent meaning; after all, if life has no meaning; neither does the emptiness people feel inside when their spirit is invalidated. Atheism is the lack of belief in the existence of a God, and I would extend that to a lack of belief in an inherent spirit as well. These two thought patterns typically accompany one another. This leads me to my biggest problem with the atheist-nihilist thought pattern: it doesn't leave you with anything; it offers no higher goal or purpose, no moral compass, no higher sense of good, no spiritual fulfillment, and no connection to the spiritual world around you.

When you recognize your inherent spiritual self and the inherent spirituality of the world around you it enables you to tap into the vast fields of love and light in the universe. When you're full of love and positivity, you're less likely to make decisions that hurt other people; in fact, over time your desires will begin to change and you'll have a strong urge to help those around you. By validating your spirituality you develop a moral compass inside of you that helps you make better decisions.

There is nothing like the feeling of real fulfilment that comes from tapping into your spirit and the spiritual realm around you. Feeling your spirit inside of you glowing and resonating with love for both yourself and others is immensely satisfying. It is difficult to make a poor decision and go against your conscience when your spirit is activated and you're actively listening to it.

This is lost on the youth of today. Somehow, in our society, we've settled on advocating for our basest natures and embracing what makes you feel good in the moment. Consequences be damned. We've reached a point in our culture where we are so far removed from the ramifications of our negative, low-vibrational actions and belief systems that we have convinced ourselves the consequences of our bad habits are unjust.

How did we get here? It's my opinion that by overly relying on emotions and what physically feels good, we've taught our generation to block their connection to their true selves, also known as their spiritual selves, the version of them that frees them from their emotionally toxic prisons. By relying entirely on emotional and physical pleasure for fulfilment rather than our true spiritual selves, we neglect the type of discipline needed for our spirits to grow. Meanwhile, our egos are growing constantly because of validation from social media and our reliance on this pleasure. Not only that but the dopamine from feeling good all the time fills your brain and satisfies you, stealing your resolve to self-improve. This growth of the ego is directly contrary to your spiritual development: the more you learn to rely on the ego, or your false self, the harder it is for you to tap into your spirit, your true self.

Spiritual deprivation this intense would make anyone depressed, anxious, and lonesome. This sense of lacking and unfulfillment in life is then amplified by our toxic habits and lack of responsibility, deepening the depression. Some people never recover, continuing to pursue the things that give them short-term pleasure, hoping that it will offer them a long-term solution to their very real emotional pain. It is my hypothesis that if we can bring culture back to the spirit and refocus our minds on improving our connection with others on a spiritual level, mental health will improve across the board. In order to do this, you must resist the temptation to chase short-term pleasure and focus on your higher goals.

Short-term pleasure is easy. It requires no commitment. If, for whatever reason, things get difficult, one can just go do something else that is easier; there is no reason to persevere for a higher purpose or goal. Why push yourself to go through difficult experiences that are required to grow if short-term pleasure is readily available? Due to the distraction of short-term pleasures, mental health problems have been amplified, as they distract us from focusing on what's truly important and give us short-term satisfaction instead of the deep spiritual fulfillment we know we need. What's worse is that deep down, even as we're distracted, we know this to be true.

This type of instant gratification is detrimental to your spiritual health and freedom, not to mention to your physical and mental health as well. This applies very well to the first example I gave of our culture's spiritual death: the pushing of pornography in pop culture. Porn is the epitome of instant gratification, also known as short-term pleasure. When you get whatever you want without working for it, that thing loses its value. This is not only a principle in psychology but also in economics.

I think of it as a matter of supply and demand. When something is readily available all the time, you're not worried about whether you'll be able to have it at a later date, making you less motivated to go after it now. This applies to pornography in a big way, as porn discourages young people from courting and interacting, not only to propagate the species but also in order to build a spiritual connection with a loving partner.

Just look at the correlation between the rise in pornography use among young men and the decline of sexually intimate relationships in Gen Z.

About 27% of men under thirty report that they haven't had sex since turning 18, according the

University of Chicago's General Social Survey, up
from 8% in 2008.
(Beschizza, 2021)

Compare this with an uptick in the percentage of young men
watching pornography by themselves from a young age:

Frequency of Viewing Pornography, By age

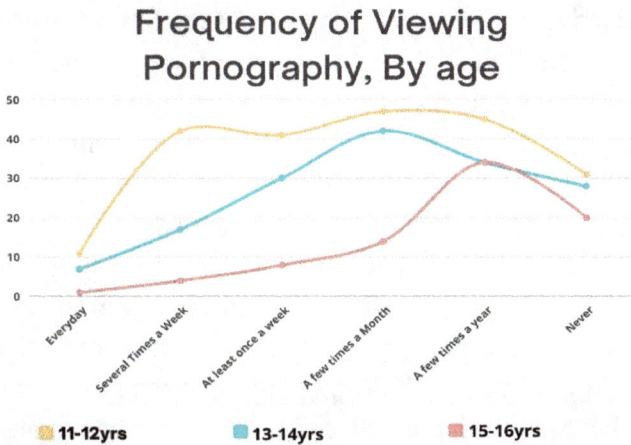

11-12yrs   13-14yrs   15-16yrs

This paper presents findings about young people's
experiences with online pornography. It draws on
data from the first national survey of secondary
school boys and girls regarding their attitudes and
feelings about online pornography, whether viewing
it deliberately or accidentally. To our knowledge, this
is the most extensive survey of 11–16 year-olds
regarding online pornography"

(Martellozzo et al, 2017)

The instant gratification of pornography has killed this
generation's natural sexual urges to interact with real people

and thus to seek out a higher relationship wherein both parties are spiritually, physically, and emotionally fulfilled. Instead, we've been brainwashed by porn to see people as objects for sexual gratification, dehumanizing them and reducing our relationships to ones in which we understand each other only in terms of how we can satisfy our urges instead of seeing each other as real people. Porn is an effective distraction from your journey toward freedom. Many people get caught in the torrent of pornography on the internet and find themselves so desensitized to sex and intimacy that they can't have a healthy relationship with their partner. Some people see porn as free, but I have to disagree. Porn is addictive, it hijacks your body's natural urges to reproduce and be intimate with another consenting adult, doing real damage to our perception of what intimacy is supposed to be, especially if you've never had sex before or if you're young and still developing. In my humble opinion, porn cheapens the incredible connection that two people feel when they're sexually engaged. In order to live spiritually free, you must free yourself from the negative perceptions and toxic life patterns you've developed around sex, love, and intimacy. Porn addiction is a real problem. If you suffer from porn addiction, find help at JoinFortify.com. Fortify is a website dedicated to helping people free themselves from porn addiction. They base their tools on real science and help individuals break free through comprehensive training, real-time analytics, and interactive support.

As you can see, clearly the lack of spirituality in our culture is causing a gaping hole in millions of people's lives. This creates a toxic chicken-and-egg scenario, as the lack of spirituality continues to be felt in our culture, people move towards short-term pleasure to achieve some sense of fulfilment. But as they continue to chase the short-term happiness that worldly pleasures such as pornography bring, they are further and further removed from their spiritual nature, and therefore from true fulfilment. As this continues, they find themselves stuck in a loop of unfulfilment. What are they using to fill the hole? Sex, drugs, and unsavoury pop culture music People have begun demeaning themselves for social points and holding themselves socially captive because they lack spiritual freedom.

In order for our culture to change, there has to be a radical shift in the way people view themselves. Seeing yourself as a spiritual being changes your self-perception in a big way. Christians have a term for this that is applicable regardless of whether you hold that faith, referring to themselves as "God's children." I like this term because it teaches self-respect in a spiritual sense. You are not just a hyper-intelligent hairless ape, as science teaches us, you are a spiritual being made by God out of pure love and light, inhabiting a physical vessel, having a human experience. That alone should warrant self-respect enough to listen to your spirit, straighten up, and fly right. It is time we all collectively look inward and accepted the spirits we all have inside of us.

Vibration and Energy

The Universe is made up of Source Energy. All
energy vibrates at a certain frequency. This means
you're vibrating at a certain frequency, and
everything you desire and don't desire is also
vibrating at a certain frequency. Vibration attracts like
vibration.
(Sincero, 2017)

Everyone is vibrating at a certain frequency, along
with every action, thought, and decision we make. When I
say "vibrating" I mean it in both a literal and spiritual sense.
Everything is vibrating in a literal sense because we're all
made up of atoms, which are made up of particles. Those
particles, aptly named "quarks" are always in a state of
vibration between other quarks and the empty space in-
between them, and because we're made out of quarks at the
subatomic level, we're also constantly vibrating as a result.

In the spiritual sense, it gets a bit more complicated.
The whole concept of spiritual vibration is based on the idea
that all matter in both the universe and ourselves is made up
of energy that vibrates at different frequencies, this vibration
is a consequence of everything having both a spiritual and
physical component to its existence. In terms of yourself, the
energy you feel vibrating inside of you is part of your
inherent spirit, also known as a soul, or as I mentioned
before, your true spiritual self.

I first encountered this idea while reading a book
titled *You are a Badass*, by Jen Sincero. There are many
books and experts on this topic; one of the most useful on the
subject of energy and vibration in my experience is a book
titled *The Energy Codes*, written by Sue Morter. Morter does
a fantastic job of breaking down the different components of
what it means to be a vibrational and energetic being.

This is useful knowledge to have because your thoughts, actions, words, and goals also have vibrational and energetic components to them. The actions that have a net positive effect on the world around you and yourself have a high vibrational frequency, while actions that are detrimental to you and your surroundings are low in vibration. By making better decisions, we raise our frequency to vibrate at a higher level. When we make poor decisions, we lower our vibration to that frequency. If you continue to make low-vibrational decisions, over time your vibration will begin to lower to that of the actions you're taking. If you want to raise your vibration, you must make higher-vibrational decisions over time. Recognizing that you have an inherent spirit allows you to take advantage of this and actively make better decisions. Remember, your inherent spirit is your true spiritual self, the real you.

Once you accept your spirituality, you won't want to participate in lower-vibrational actions anymore. You'll begin to feel that there is a higher purpose for your existence and a real reason to elevate yourself through discipline and hard work. When you connect to your spirit, you will realize that there is an infinite amount of love all around you waiting for you to call it your way, which will remove your need for group validation and give you a sense of security in your own self-love. The freedom you feel when you are no longer beholden to the group and entirely beholden to your inner spirit for validation is immeasurable.

Why is accepting your spirit such a good feeling? Because you've accepted your true self. This helps you fulfill your higher purpose, as you have a much clearer understanding of what you're supposed to be doing. It also helps your mental health because you finally feel accepted and recognize that you are loved infinitely, even as you are.

Over time, you'll begin to phase the lower-vibrational pastimes out of your life. You will soon discover after connecting with your inner spirit that you don't want to participate in low-vibrational and base activities. Once you become attuned to your vibrational frequency, and you see that there is no ceiling for growth, you won't want to do things that distract you from bettering yourself. You will recognize that the lower-vibrational way of life was killing you, it was holding you back and distracting you from your real purpose.

You will recognize that it was *you* who put the chains around your hands and feet and bound you to stay where you were. Your spirit enables you to free yourself from this imprisonment by creating space between you and your actions, allowing you to make better decisions.

In our culture today, so many people are stuck stumbling around in the dark, bound in chains of their own making. This is because of their refusal to look inside of themselves and to be honest about their higher sense of being and the higher sense of morality that accompanies it. These people will tend to feel both their true spiritual self and the higher moral law that precedes it, and actively repress both. They're afraid because to listen to your inner spirit calling you to greatness also means taking responsibility for yourself and what you say and do. This means that you can no longer operate in a morally gray area, that all of your actions have consequences, that absolute truth exists, and that the only judgment worth truly caring about is whether your spirit truly feels something is morally acceptable.

As discussed in Chapter One, absolute truth is real. This has direct consequences for morality and ethics. When something is inherently good, it has a higher vibration associated with it and is considered a net positive. When something is inherently bad, however, it is associated with negative and low vibrations. This is the effect of absolute truth on a spiritual level: some actions are morally benevolent, others reprehensible.

This idea originated in ancient Hinduism from the law of Karma. Karma in Hinduism is the basic law of cause and effect, stating that benevolent and beneficial actions will lead to beneficial effects, and that harmful actions will lead to harmful effects. Applying this to the spiritual domain, high- and positive-vibrational actions will bring positive results, and negative, low-vibrational actions will bring negative results. This concept of manifesting through our actions is another iteration of the law of attraction that we discussed earlier in Chapter 2. By recognizing that our actions have an energetic component to them, we're able to raise our vibration through concentrated effort.

When you do something, it has an effect, as we saw in the previous chapter when discussing the law of attraction. The more you do something, the more likely you are to attract that same behaviour in your life. Thus, when you engage in low-vibrational actions that are damaging to the spirit, you actively hinder your spiritual progress and you put more roadblocks in your way down the line. Not only that but over time, whether you realize it or not, you will begin to resent yourself.

The biggest problem with this is it's almost impossible to feel truly worthy of love in its highest form if you loathe yourself, the actions you take, or things you say or stand for. This is because you feel on a fundamental level that these actions or stances deny your true spirit. The only real solution is to start changing your actions little by little to improve yourself. By attending to your spirit as a sort of barometer for your actions, you can determine what is best at any given moment. Through incremental change, as discussed in Chapter One, we are able to establish a real sense of self-love, which has a tangible impact on our ability to connect with others, both in the spiritual sense and in the physical and mental.

If you're depriving yourself of self-love, I'd argue that you're also depriving yourself of love from those around you trying to send it your way. This robs you of the joy of receiving love, the most powerful energy in the universe, and blocks those around you from the joy of giving it.

Love is the most powerful force in the universe. It can melt through hate, anger, despair, and all negativity. But the difficulty here is that if you don't allow self-love into your life, you prevent yourself from feeling the majority of love in general. Loving yourself is the secret to allowing love from others into your life. The spirit enables self-love on an energetic level. Love has both a physical effect as a result of chemicals in the brain, and an energetic one through the high vibration associated with it. By recognizing your true spiritual self, you allow yourself to take advantage of the high vibration associated with love. Connecting with your spiritual self, and recognizing that at your core you are a spiritual being, allows you to love yourself unconditionally, even as flawed as we all are. By tapping into the inherent spirit inside of us, we are able to feel a sense of love for ourselves that can help us improve our flaws and our self-perception.

Self-love is integral to freedom in every sense of the word. Unless you see yourself as worthy of self-love, you cannot see yourself as worthy of love from others or the universe, and you'll begin to consider yourself unworthy of the inherent freedoms you possess. If you desire to be truly free, you must free yourself from self-hatred. Hatred binds, enslaves, and murders. It is by channeling hatred and the negative aspects of our humanity on an energetic and vibrational level that people are drawn to commit evil and morally reprehensible actions against others. By channeling self-love, we ease the hatred in our hearts toward others and feel a sense of contentment with the life we have. Even if you're not where you want to be, you're thankful for being where you are in the moment.

You have to allow yourself forgiveness for your imperfections. The spirit is what enables forgiveness for both yourself and others on an energetic level. When we give forgiveness and patience to someone, we allow healing love into their lives. This applies to your interactions both with yourself and with other people; seeing life through a spiritual lens allows for love in spite of our human nature.

Of course, the topics in previous chapters also play a role in the art of self-love and spiritual freedom. You must love yourself enough to discipline yourself to do what is right, not what is easy. You must adopt a rigid mindset in order to not give in to base, low-vibrational desires. As you pour more and more time and effort into your spiritual development, these disciplines will come more naturally and you will find it easier to choose higher-vibrational pastimes. Once the habit sticks and the uncomfortable adjustment period is over, you won't want to go back because you'll be living in a spiritually, mentally, and emotionally fulfilled world, in which your desires are actively changing to help you reach your highest potential net good. When you focus on magnifying good, the law of attraction dictates that the good in your life will be amplified. Focus on the good.

Remember, once we start operating out of our spirits rather than our egos, we align with our true selves. Our ego is a protective personality. When we are born, we are small and have little control over the world, so as a natural defense mechanism, we develop a protective personality to keep us safe while we grow. However, operating only within the established imaginative frameworks of the mind seriously inhibits your ability to reach your true potential. Your spirit is connected to all of the wisdom in the universe from its direct connection with God because of the concept of source energy, and because energy can never be destroyed, it's existed for much longer than your body has and will continue to exist long after your body fades away. Your spirit has a lot of inherent wisdom, and its connection to the larger universe has virtually limitless potential. Because of source energy (some call this God, and the Judaeo-Christian school of thought calls this the Holy spirit), our spirits, the energetic components of our being, have a direct link to this divine energy. If source energy is the sum of all energy in the universe, we would automatically be connected to that energy source because we're energetic beings.

In order to access that awesome knowledge, we have to accept ourselves as we are, including all our flaws, and recognize that we're imperfect humans. This is where our spirits come into play. You see, our egos can't handle that type of direct, open criticism of the fragility of our existence, so instead, our egos defensively come up with any excuse they can in order to feel superior and to defend our reason for existing.

When you give yourself self-love, the ego is calmed because the spirit reminds the ego that its existence is temporary and that the ego and the mind are an illusion. You are reminded that your core essence is pure love and light energy. It is unnecessary to constantly stress out about ego fragility because you love yourself enough already as you are. You've given yourself permission to feel the love in the universe around you and the inherent love your spirit carries inside of you. You no longer feel the need to judge yourself harshly or look outside of yourself for fulfillment.

You may start to see yourself from a third-person perspective, creating space between you and your actions and allowing you to make better decisions and feel less emotionally attached to every little thing. This allows for more feelings of joy in the moment and resilience towards adversity. After all, if you are less emotionally attached to your decisions, you can see more clearly the influx of negativity from poor decisions and discipline yourself in the areas of life in which you struggle.

The reason your resilience to adversity improves with spiritual growth and ego detachment is rather obvious: you're able to see things clearly without the distractions of the world and your ever-present mind. Because the ego is manifested in your mind rather than your spirit, when we focus on the ego more intensely than the spirit we open ourselves up to overthinking, anxiety, depression, and general unhappiness as by-products. The stress of being overly emotionally attached to life and feeling a sense of being lost is a symptom of the unchecked ego and a lack of connection to your spirituality. Once you open up a connection to your spirit, you allow the healing process to begin. Not only that but you will actively start making decisions from a spiritual perspective rather than a mental one. This is what allows for more space between you and your decisions.

Your spirit is eternal energy that can never be destroyed because it's pure energy. Remember, energy can never be destroyed, only transformed. This is the first law of thermodynamics, and it affects the spiritual existence we all experience in a big way. Because we are all energy beings with an inherent soul, the first law of thermodynamics dictates that we existed before life in the spiritual form and will continue to exist after life. When you look at things from this perspective the trifles of everyday life don't seem nearly as significant, allowing you to relax into yourself and feel gratitude for your current circumstances instead of disdain, which in turn puts the law of attraction to work *for* you and not *against* you. All of these important principles about spirituality are absent from our culture today, leading to what I call the mental health crisis in America.

It's no secret that depression and anxiety are on the rise in the United States. It shouldn't be a surprise that as our culture loses its sense of spirituality, mental health continues to grow worse.

In 2019, just prior to the COVID-19 pandemic, 19.86% of adults experienced a mental illness, equivalent to nearly 50 million Americans.

Suicidal ideation continues to increase among adults in the U.S. 4.58% of adults report having serious thoughts of suicide, an increase of 664,000 people from last year's dataset. The national rate of suicidal ideation among adults has increased every year since 2011–2012. This was a larger increase than seen in [2021's] report and is a concerning trend to see going into the COVID-19 pandemic.

A growing percentage of youth in the U.S. live with major depression. 15.08% of youth experienced a major depressive episode in the past year, a 1.24% increase from last year's dataset. In the bottom-ranked states, up to 19% of youth ages 12–17 experienced major depression.

(Mental Health America, 2022)

Connecting to the spirit can help ease many of life's burdens. It is by feeling the inherent self-love of our inner spirits that we heal this sickness in our culture.

Miller made a 10-year follow-up study on depressed mothers and their offspring and reported that maternal religiosity and mother–child concordance in religiosity were protective against depression in the offspring. They also reported that low levels of religiosity were associated with substance abuse in the offspring.
(Verghese, 2008)

A lack of spirituality in your life can lead to depression, substance abuse, and emotional pain. In a culture that has embraced this spiritual genocide, mental health issues will continue to increase. The spirit is what allows you to access and feel love. Without a connection to it, life seems bleak and insignificant. Feeling a connection to your spirit actively helps you make better decisions in your day-to-day life. Not only that but by connecting to the spirit our egos are freed to focus solely on the ego's role, which is instinctual protection, not higher fulfillment. You will never find true fulfillment through a protective personality. It is only by accepting your spiritual existence that you free yourself from the self-hatred all humans have felt for being imperfect.

The steps leading to self-acceptance can leave you feeling vulnerable. It's important to note that vulnerability and weakness are not the same things: It is a weakness to avoid accepting yourself. It takes real strength to be vulnerable. Of course, there are circumstances in which being publicly vulnerable is a bad strategy, but that doesn't mean that being vulnerable is a weakness.

Once you've recognized that you are a spiritual being, there is another level to strive for, and I find this to be the most difficult, requiring a lifetime to truly understand and master. What I am referring to is the dissolution of the ego into the shared consciousness and the collective pool of knowledge that exists around us.

As best I can describe it, collective consciousness looks something like this: when one person works on themselves spiritually, everyone around them can feel and benefit from the love they pull in from the universe and the positive energy that they're putting into their lives. The principle not only applies on a practical, physical level (that is, benefiting from better interactions between people) but also on a spiritual and energetic level, through interaction or just through proximity. When you are attuned to your spiritual self and tapping into the collective consciousness, people around you will begin to take notice, some may even comment that you have a light about you, but everyone will benefit from being around you because when you interact with someone who has a higher vibration it raises your own.

Thich Nhat Hauh was a Vietnamese Thiền Buddhist monk, an advocate for peace, an author, a teacher, and he was recognized as the main inspiration for engaged Buddhism. Recognized as the "father of mindfulness", Nhất Hạnh's teachings are still influencing Western practices of Buddhism today, even after his death in January of 2022. It was his idea that every realm of being was a result of the collective consciousness of those inside it. If the world around us is peaceful and happy place, it's from the collective conscious of those living there. However, if it's burning down, we are all considered co-responsible for the damage. In his words

Whether a place is pleasant or unpleasant always depends upon the collective consciousness of its inhabitants.

(Nhất Hạnh, Thích, and Neumann, 2008)

The basic idea that I've grasped from it is very similar to the concept of self-elevation (and subsequent benefit) through hard work. When you benefit from this labour, the people around you also benefit. When you raise yourself as a member of the community, the whole community gets to rise a little with you. The same applies here, but on an energetic and spiritual basis.

Because people interact on a spiritual level as well as on the physical and mental/emotional levels, being in proximity to and interacting with people who have higher vibrations than yourself is a great way to jump-start your spiritual growth. When you interact, you share energy. When you walk past someone in the street, you share energy. When you look at someone, you share energy. Everything is energy, and thus every action has an energetic, vibrational component. Energy transference is something that happens automatically, and it is so fundamental to our existence as humans that most people scarcely realize that they're doing it. Have you ever been having a great day and felt really good, and then suddenly, after interacting with someone who was negative, you felt drained? This is an example of people sharing energy at an unconscious level. One minute you're great, but after you shared energy with the negative person, your joy began to shrink.

By this logic, it stands to reason that every being has a sphere of energy they can immediately influence around them. When two people interact, they momentarily share that sphere; when this happens, one of two things occurs: either the person with the lower vibration is elevated or the person with the higher vibration is lowered.

This is much like when two people walk down a street together. If their intent is to walk together, either one person slows down or the other person speeds up. The difference, in this case, is that if you are the lower-vibrational person, and if your intent is to learn, you can tap into the collective consciousness around you and the higher-vibrational individual in order to try and elevate yourself with them. This works because the more love you bring into your life, the more positive energy you actively send out. If someone is vibrating at a higher level than you, and you'd like to humble yourself before them in order to learn, if they accept, your goal is not only to acquire mental knowledge about certain skills but to raise your spiritual attunement and vibration as close to their level as possible by absorbing the love and positive energy they put out as a byproduct of bettering themselves.

Energy is a fluid thing. If you are not actively working on raising your vibration and interacting with high-vibrational people, over time you will attract lower-vibrational people and habits into your life.

This applies to large groups as well; cities, massive metro areas, states, and countries, anywhere that people are united. These groups of people can pool their energy together to push an idea, thought, or emotion, positive or negative, benevolent or malicious, using the collective energy of the group. As we'll discuss in the fifth chapter, this can be very damaging to your freedom if people are not aware that they're participating due to being disconnected from the power of their spirits. Everyone's decisions affect the energy of the group around them. When two people are fighting in a room of ten, the other eight naturally and quickly see the negative effects of that bad energy and either start to move away from the tension, try to send positivity to help ease the tension, or give into the negativity they feel and propagate even more of it around them.

The collective consciousness is what allows us to make our world heaven or hell. Even when applying the principles of the collective consciousness and being aware of the energy you put out affecting the group, whether you are living a positive or negative life always comes down to the individual. Individual responsibility and freedom are the only paths toward a spiritually free and healthy culture.

People feel positivity and change in general at a spiritual level. Everything in life has a spiritual component, and this requires recognizing that we and everything around us are all part of the spiritual collective that is either benefiting us or adding to the negativity around us based on the decisions of its occupants.

It's very surprising how quickly people pick up on the energy around them. Humans evolved spiritual instincts to be aware of energy the same way they evolved their physical ones in order to catch dinner. Negative spiritual energy can be detrimental to our health, and often people who have negative energies also experience a negative impact on their longevity and wellbeing. This is why we've evolved our spiritual instincts to combat the threats of others' negativity, strengthening ourselves against their spiritual attacks with our own self-love and self-reliance. We can love ourselves as we are and accept our flaws as physical beings by connecting to our true spiritual selves and ceasing to rely on the ego. In addition, by filling ourselves with love drawn from the universe, we leave no room for others' negativity to seep into our lives. There will never be a shortage of love for you to fill your life with.

Existing in a spiritual collective consciousness means that there's always going to be more love than you could ever hope to need; an infinite amount of love is actively waiting for you to call on it. It means that you'll never be alone, because you're connected to everything and everyone through the spiritual collective.

Recent psychological findings from Johnathan Haidt, an American social scientist and author, suggest that our brains are hardwired to work both for our own benefit *and* for the benefit of the collective. While this doesn't prove the existence of the collective consciousness, it better outlines the physical circuitry in our brains associated with spiritual phenomenon. In his book *The Righteous Mind*, Haidt says:

I suggested that human nature is 90 percent chimp and 10 percent bee. We are like chimps in being primates whose minds were shaped by the relentless competition of individuals with their neighbors. We are descended from a long string of winners in the game of social life. This is why we are Glauconians, usually more concerned about the appearance of virtue than the reality (as in Glaucon's story about the ring of Gyges).

But human nature also has a more recent groupish overlay. We are like bees in being ultrasocial creatures whose minds were shaped by the relentless competition of groups with other groups. We are descended from earlier humans whose groupish minds helped them cohere, cooperate, and outcompete other groups. That doesn't mean that our ancestors were mindless or unconditional team players; it means they were selective. Under the right conditions, they were able to enter a mind-set of "one for all, all for one" in which they were truly working for the good of the group, and not just for their own advancement within the group.

My hypothesis ... is that human beings are conditional hive creatures. We have the ability (under special conditions) to transcend self-interest and lose ourselves (temporarily and ecstatically) in something larger than ourselves. That ability is what I'm calling the hive switch . The hive switch, I propose, is a group-related adaptation that can only be explained "by a theory of between-group selection," as [George C. Williams] said. It cannot be explained by selection at the individual level. (How would this strange ability help a person to outcompete his neighbors in the same group?) The hive switch is an adaptation for making groups more cohesive, and therefore more successful in competition with other groups.

If the hive hypothesis is true, then it has enormous implications for how we should design organizations, study religion, and search for meaning and joy in our lives. Is it true? Is there really a hive switch?
(Haidt, 2013, p. 228)

This means that on a physical level, there's circuitry in place that benefits us when we work together as a group. We are literally hardwired for working together as a collective group toward common goals in certain circumstances. It is my assertion that this applies to the spiritual level as well to forms of energies being exchanged as discussed earlier.

Being connected to everything and waking up to the collective spirituality of humanity is great and all, but what does it have to do with living a free life today? Everything.

Being connected to the spiritual collective consciousness is one of the most liberating experiences one can have in this lifetime. Not to mention that it is from our spirits that our desire to be free originates. Our spirits want us to live a life in which we are free from low-vibrational lifestyles. In order to do this, we must listen to their direction. To follow your inner spirit regardless of popular opinion is to speak truth to power; that is freedom, and it manifests from the spirit.

Another reason being connected to the collective consciousness is beneficial to your freedom is that it allows you to live fully and freely with the world and to spread all the love you feel for the world to everyone around you. When you do that, you're giving love. When you give, you create a vacuum. That vacuum then has to be filled by the universe with more love and blessings. Knowing that you'll always get more than you give to others is a powerful tool for the magnification of love. These blessings and that love are given to you through the same collective consciousness through which you sent the love out in the first place.

By giving and participating in the collective trade of spiritual energy, you give yourself access to the unlimited blessings in the universe. By consciously recognizing that every action has a spiritual vibration, and that subsequently that vibration affects you and the collective spiritual energy of the world around you, you can actively make choices that raise your vibration. In response to this, the vibration of your environment, of those around you, and of your actions will all be amplified.

The world is actively adapting to the vibrational frequencies of your actions. When you raise the frequency of your actions, over time the vibration of your surroundings will rise, meaning that you'll naturally attract that bigger house, that nicer car, that sexy life partner, and those solid friends. Getting what you want is entirely dependent on what you're willing to ask the universe for and on its frequency in relation to your own.

If you're asking for something that's vibrating at a frequency so high it doesn't even register, meaning that you're actions are vibrating at a much lower level than the thing you want, you need to train yourself to make higher-vibrational choices in order to elevate yourself spiritually to the frequency of the thing you want. It's not going to happen overnight, but it will happen. Sometimes you notice the changes instantly. Once you make a decision to stick to a higher way of living, to elevate yourself with love and recognize and nourish your spirit, the higher vibrations will come naturally. You have to listen to your spirit, not your ego. Your spirit will tell you what it needs to grow; listen to it and it will guide you with all the wisdom of the connected universe toward your life's purpose.

If you're at all curious to learn more about bioenergetics, the study of the transformation of energy in living organisms, please listen to or read *The Energy Codes* by Dr. Sue Morton. It's a great read and one that has helped me greatly on my own spiritual journey. If you'd like to learn more, I've included a complete list of references in the bibliography at the back of this book.

I could go on for a lifetime about the benefits of tapping into your inherent spirituality and awakening to the collective spiritual consciousness and energy, but I'll leave more detailed description to those more engrossed in the subject and with more experience and better-articulated opinions.

You may be wondering why I haven't tied God into the spiritual discussion very much, and that's because I'm saving my discussion of God for Chapter Four. Regardless of whether you believe in God, I find that most people are willing to accept that they do have some spiritual aspect to them, even if they are numb to it. There will always be those who cling to the ego and never admit to their true spiritual nature. I would argue that one of the reasons atheists and nihilists deny their spiritual nature is because to accept the spirit is to accept the existence of God (but more on this in Chapter Four). For atheists, it's pretty obvious that they reject the idea of a spirit, but nihilists are just as quick to reject their inherent spirituality. Nihilism teaches that nothing matters and that therefore there are no morals. Your spirit is your moral barometer, remember? By rejecting the spirit, nihilists are able to continue the destructive thought pattern that says their actions and the morality they feel within themselves are inherently meaningless, rather than listening to their spirits telling them the opposite is true.

In relation to the spiritual lifestyle, the correlation between morality and ethics is very positive. As I said above, the more we are connected to our spiritual selves, and by extension the better we are able to feel others' spiritual health, the more we become connected to other people. It's much harder to make poor ethical decisions when you're spiritually connected to everyone who'd be hurt by your bad choice.

In many movies, the protagonists are given arcs that see them realize the error of their ways (often called the 'come to Jesus' moment). If they manage to fix the problem and things return to normal, they usually have a better spiritual connection to their surroundings, appreciating both their environment and the people around them. This usually results in the protagonist making better decisions than before, and possibly helping the people they were ignoring.

Ebenezer Scrooge is a perfect example. In *A Christmas Carol* by Charles Dickens, the protagonist Scrooge is a cheapskate who refuses to pay his workers well and loses the love of his life by chasing money. On the night before Christmas, Scrooge is visited by three ghosts who take him to his past, present, and future Christmases, laying out for him to see clearly that he drove away everyone he loved.

Scrooge is in denial until the last ghost (the Ghost of Christmas Yet to Come) takes him to his future grave, where he sees that his death is not mourned by anybody and that all of the efforts he put into gathering wealth were all for nothing because he lacked a spiritual connection with others. He also watches the crippled child of one of his employees die because they couldn't afford the medicine the child needed due to the low wages Scrooge was paying them. The shock of this scares Scrooge so much that he begs the spirits to give him another chance at life.

He wakes up the next morning and it's Christmas Day. Scrooge, with his new lease on life, is now more spiritually connected to the community. He's woken up to the significance of charity and helping those in need, but also to the importance of nourishing his own spirituality. After he realizes that he was actively hurting people with his selfishness, he changes his ways. The first thing he does is buy the biggest turkey at the market and have it sent to his employee's house, and later he gives that same employee a raise, with the explicit understanding that it is to buy medicine for the sickly child. He acts so differently, so suddenly, because his spirit had been ignited; he realizes that he is a spiritual being having a human experience. It's of course also true that Scrooge wanted to save himself from the consequences of his actions, as there were depictions in the book of brutal punishments for his money-grubbing ways. But Scrooge is said to have opened his heart with love. Could his intentions have been pure, based on a desire to help those he felt spiritually connected to after doing them so much damage?

When you become spiritually dead, you become a Scrooge. You shut yourself off from the love around you and the harm you're causing to others. When you're spiritually open and attuned, you can make better, higher-vibrational decisions because you can better see and feel the ramifications of your actions on a spiritual level.

The spiritual lens that every person is able to look through is encoded with an inherent decision-making hierarchy designed to net you the best moral positive and ethical good possible. The problem with this is that our spirits are morally pure but our bodies and egos are definitely not, and all three have a pull in our decision-making. Looking at life through a spiritual lens means making hard decisions, delaying gratification, maintaining unpopular opinions, keeping your mind and body in check and at the behest of the spirit, and very often going against the grain of the spiritually dead world.

Commanding the mind and body to listen to the spirit is a daily decision, and it's never easy. No one is perfect. Listening to the spirit is a skill that every human can cultivate and over time, with some practice, improve upon. Eventually, it will become a habit like everything else, due to the neuroplastic aspects of your brain that we discussed in Chapter One.

The spiritual lens is hard to look through because it shows everything plainly. All of our issues, all of the negative attributes in our lives, and all the negative energy-draining people around us who we believe to be our friends are clearly visible to us when we look at life through the spiritual lens. This can at times be crushing for the ego. Honesty can be hard to swallow, but it's the best medicine for healing your life. Your spirit will never lie to you, so if you have an intuition about something or you feel that you need to make a change in your life, listen to your spirit for guidance. By looking at life through the spiritual lens, we are able to see what's truly important.

Gratitude is a big part of spirituality, especially if you feel like you have nothing to be grateful for. When feelings of despair take over, that's when you most need the shining light of gratitude. In order to attract what you want into your life, you need to focus on being grateful and taking care of what you already have, not on your problems and the negativity around you. If you focus on the negative, you'll just attract more of it. When you are struggling and you feel like it is for nothing, that's when you should make gratitude the top priority in your life. Count your blessings!

Viktor Frankl, a psychiatrist, philosopher, and holocaust survivor wrote a book titled *Man's Search for Meaning*, in which he describes in detail the horrors of the concentration camps he survived in Nazi Germany. It's a heartbreaking book, but one that is absolutely necessary in order to understand the importance of gratitude and the spirit. During his time in the camps, Dr. Frankl wrote,

In some ways suffering ceases to be suffering at the moment it finds a meaning, such as the meaning of a sacrifice.
(Frankl, 2017)

During one of the worst atrocities in recorded history, with a totalitarian boot being pressed on their necks and while seeing his people being murdered in mass numbers, Dr. Frankl spoke of finding meaning and gratitude in life in order to bear the suffering.

Everything can be taken from a man but one thing: the last of the human freedoms—to choose one's attitude in any given set of circumstances, to choose one's own way.
(Frankl, 2017)

If you feel stuck, or like you have nothing to be grateful for, remember that you have a choice in the way you view your circumstances. In order to overcome the adversity in your life and truly live freely, you must live a life of gratitude.

Gratitude fortifies the spirit. It reminds you that there is always a joy to offset tragedy. Living a life of gratitude motivates us even more to be responsible stewards of our surroundings. When we are grateful for something, we automatically have a stronger desire to take better care of it. This is mainly because we want to show our gratitude.

If you're at a point where you feel you have nothing to be grateful for, you need to connect with your inner spirit. Not only will your spirit give you guidance toward a better life but it will give you a direct connection to all of the love and gratitude in the universe due to the collective consciousness.

If you feel like you don't have a reason to be grateful, your spirit will give you one. Once you connect to your innate spiritual nature, you'll have access to plenty of gratitude. Once you have that gratitude, magnify it. As you increase your gratitude on a spiritual level, you are making room for more blessings. By extending your gratitude, you're also extending your realm of stewardship.

That space should then be filled to the brim with service. Service is one of the most important things we as humans can ever do. The Bible says that "faith without deeds is dead" (James 2:26) There's no reason for the universe to give you love and blessings if you're not going to share them with those around you. By looking outside of ourselves, we are able to broaden our perspective in every sense of the word and expand the blessings we receive.

This is the spiritual system for blessings: gratitude makes the space for blessings and positivity to come into your life by magnifying all the good you already have. You then put that good energy to work by helping people, which in turn creates more to be grateful for and more space in which for that gratitude to reside. This in turn increases the amount you can serve, which increases your personal blessings. It is an endless cycle that can be used to great success. I remember this principle with the mantra "The more you give, the more you get." If you were completely shut off from your spirituality, you'd be unaware of the spiritual transactions taking place.

Gratitude is vital to freedom. In a literal sense, it allows us to see why we have it so good when we're living freely, and it motivates us to maintain the habits that perpetuate that lifestyle. In a spiritual sense, It allows us to draw closer to our divine self, magnifying our positivity, raising our vibration, and bringing more love into our lives. Gratitude is something that tends to change people's perspectives.

Everyone has had moments in life when they lose or almost lose something they care about. When this happens, you recognize just how valuable that thing is to you. Why was your perception of that thing's value different before the loss (or near loss) as opposed to after? Because before you lacked gratitude. Now that the full scope of that thing's value has been brought into plain view, you are forced to grieve the loss and recognize your full gratitude for it.

Have you ever noticed how people usually only say nice things about the deceased, especially at funerals? Obviously it would be rude to say something mean to a grieving person about their departed loved one, and some cultures have superstitions about speaking ill of the dead. But on a spiritual level, when someone dies, their energy is much less perceptible. When their spirit leaves their body, we feel the full lack of their energy. We can't connect with them on an energetic level, and this hurts our spirits because we cared for them and we truly miss that connection. They are not gone, but unless you're some type of psychic (the existence of whom I have no interest in debating one way or the other), you feel cut off. Getting cut off hurts. To heal the spiritual wound their energy's departure has left, we use the gratitude we have for them and the love we shared for them to grieve.

Gratitude is the ultimate healer.

Gratitude is one of the most powerful tools we have in our arsenal for spiritual freedom from both negativity and captivity to the ego. When we are grateful, we can finally let go.

In conclusion, the spirit is vital to freedom. Without a connection to our spiritual selves, we remain in the cycle of self-hatred and ego-reliance. The only way to live a free and fulfilling life is by validating your inner spirit and listening to its guidance rather than seeking validation from an outside source. The spirit connects you to a vast landscape of love and positivity, which you can then use to better your own life and raise your internal vibration. It enables a spiritual connection with others as well as a spiritual trade between those people. The spirit enables the power of gratitude to fully activate in life, allowing you to manifest your dreams in reality.

It is through the spirit that we find true connection and love in this lifetime, and by culturally removing it we have taken away valuable tools with which the next generation could find true fulfilment in their lives. It is time our culture brought the spirit back into the conversation. Embrace your spirit, embrace love, and embrace freedom.

Chapter 4: God, Psychedelics, and the Meaning of Life

How does a finite being like me even begin to define the infinite? God is big. Really big. So big in fact that you can spend your entire life contemplating just how big God is and still not wrap your head around it. The existence of a divine creator who bestows our freedoms upon us is an essential clarifying point in the debate regarding freedom today. When the US Constitution was originally written, its authors truly believed that our rights were granted to us by God and not by the government. This is an important distinction in the hierarchy of power when it comes to your freedoms and liberties. God grants you your freedoms, not the government, meaning that the government has no ground to stand on when it attempts to legislate your God-given rights away.

When I say "God," I don't mean it in the Christian sense. Although I personally believe in Christ and one omnipotent God, as long as you believe your freedoms are granted to you by an outside force other than governmental or human organizational bodies in general, the concept of having divine natural rights still applies. For the sake of this argument, you can have the concept of God take whatever form feels natural to you. When speaking about God, I am not implying any sort of organized religion, nor am I advocating for one. Organized religion has a rather colorful history in relation to freedom. While not inherently bad, organized religion has in the past led to a reduction in freedom of thought through abuses of power. Although organized religion has many positive aspects to it, it has also led to priestcraft, which is the practice of priests using their offices to intervene in their congregations' personal relationship with God.

Organized religion has been used throughout history to control the masses by putting a priest between people and God to prevent their having a direct relationship. A clear example of this would be the Catholic Church's refusal during the dark ages to translate the Bible from Latin into the common tongue. The church needed its parishioners to be reliant on the priests to translate the holy texts for them. Once the Bible was in the hands of the common man, they could learn morality from the book on their own without the priests spoon-feeding them. This was hugely detrimental to the Catholic Church, as many of their teachings at the time had no basis in the Bible, such as the indulgence system put in place for priests to sell vouchers supposedly allowing people to get out of hell.

"These indulgences not only bestowed pardon for sins committed already, they were used to license the commission of future transgressions as well."

91

(Brown, 2017)

The goal of the Church at the time wasn't to share God's love and positive energy; it was about controlling the masses. When they controlled the holy texts, each member of the church was entirely dependent on the priests in order to learn about God.

When this happens, organizations begin to take the place of God. When humans or organizations attempt to replace God in a given culture, the results are always disastrous, and it makes people skeptical of the concept of a god in general. Countless examples, from the Spanish Inquisition to the Protestant Reformation, the Salem witch trials, the Protestant anti-technology movement, and Islamic extremism and terrorism, have all left a sour taste in many people's mouths regarding the subject of organized religion.

Using the example of the Catholic Church during the dark ages, we can extract a few real and visceral lessons regarding what happens when an organization takes the place of God. Below is just one example of the atrocities that occurred in the Roman Catholic Church when priestcraft was being practiced.

From the birth of Popery in 606 to the present time, it is estimated by careful and credible historians, that more than fifty millions of the human family, have been slaughtered for the crime of heresy by popish persecutors, an average of more than forty thousand religious murders for every year of the existence of popery.
(Dowling, 1849, pp. 541–542)

Here's the kicker: the concept of God doesn't have to be tied to any organized religion. Instead, I advocate for each person to go out and cultivate a personal relationship with God independent of religious groups, even if you're religious. By detaching the concept of God from your religious organization, you allow yourself to see God outside of human organizational structures, creating the opportunity for you to take an energetic perspective, one based on a real relationship between God's energy and your own, rather than a religious one that may be negatively affected by other imperfect humans in your religious group.

This is an important concept, as seeing God at an energetic level allows you to empathize with those with whom you disagree rather than disdain them. Of course, I'm not saying you should abandon your faith. I'm merely suggesting that, in my humble opinion, God operates on an energetic level, and that organized religion typically acts to interpret that energy in a way normal working-class people can understand without having to dedicate their lives to study. This can be extremely beneficial, especially if you want a greater connection with God in your day-to-day life.

The opportunity to be around like-minded people in a community that looks after its members is one of the best aspects of organized religion. I'm not saying being religious is necessarily a bad thing, only that, as with politics, people can get carried away, with groupthink eventually leading to the death of individual thought.

Humans are flawed creatures. Our interpretations are often wrong. Looking at God through an energetic lens rather than a religious one allows for imperfect people with imperfect views to have a relationship with this perfect being.

God is real, and having a real relationship with God is a direct path to freedom. In Chapter Three we discussed how being in proximity to someone with a higher vibration can raise your own; the same holds true for God, but on an infinitely grander scale. God is the highest vibrating being in the universe. By inviting God into your life and seeking God out, you raise your vibration the same way you would if you were around other higher-vibration people. The difference is that it's much more powerful and effective. God is infinitely wiser than we are, and by inviting God into our lives we invite all of the wisdom and love that accompanies him. Some see God as source energy, that whereby all energy comes flowing into the universe.

[Source energy] is simply a vibration of love, of wholeness, of completion. In that energy you feel complete and at peace, there is nothing you have to do or prove or become. It is just a state of peace that you relax into when you connect with Source/God. (Smith, 2015)

God is the reason we have the freedoms we do. Many secular atheist types like to argue against the existence of God, never giving a second thought to how the existence of God is beneficial to their lives. The idea of human rights is a relatively new one, stemming from the Judeo-Christian faith, on which Western morality happens to be based. It is from a perspective that sees every human as God's creation that the idea of natural inalienable rights first appeared.

For Christian churches, there is no doubt about the existence of immanent natural rights. Theological thought incorporated the idea that natural rights are of religious and divine origin and Christianity has assumed that this is true for centuries.

(Zuber, 2019)

Whether you believe in God or not, you've certainly benefited from God's existence. You don't have to be aware of God or His works to benefit from them on a daily basis. God granted you the desire you have in your soul to be free in the first place, as it was God that created your soul. I mentioned in Chapter Three that to deny the spirit is to deny God. This is because your spirit is a direct connection to God and God's love. By embracing the spirit, you embrace your connection with God. By denying it, you deny not only your true self but your lifeline to the divine. By denying your spirit, you deny yourself the ability to operate on an energetic level and receive blessings from God through the law of attraction.

Too many times throughout history we have seen what happens to a country when God is removed from the equation and a ruler or government is placed in his stead. Akin to the way religious organizations took the place of God in the dark ages, rulers and governments can also take the place of God in the eyes of the people. God's replacement leads to the death of individual thought and expression and always toward a totalitarian regime. When the government attempts to take the place of God, the imperfect views of those running it will inevitably seep down into their policies, which always end up harming the lower classes. Once this happens, freedom no longer exists in the rule of law. In the twentieth century alone we saw too many examples of what it looks like when a totalitarian government takes the place of God. The Soviet Union and Nazi Germany, as well as modern day China, are perfect examples of the atrocities committed by those who take the place of God.

The Soviet Union began its prosecution of millions of innocent citizens under a communist dictatorship in 1917. There were 61,911,000 total victims over its reign from 1917–1987. Those victims were displaced and sent to disturbing living conditions where many of them died.
(Rummel, 1990)

Stalin sent millions of people to the Gulags, a form of internment camp with horrifying conditions. If you ever want a look into the suffering of the Russian people, listen to or read *The Gulag Archipelago* by Aleksandr Solzhenitsyn. It is the heart-breaking account of a man who survived the camps himself and used his photographic memory to perfectly describe the horrors he had to endure. As he said in the book:

Unlimited power in the hands of limited people always leads to cruelty.
(Solzhenitsÿn et al, 2018)

During the reign of the Soviet Union, the government went zealously prosecuted its own innocent people. Citizens who did nothing wrong were rounded up in the middle of the night and told that they were under arrest, often being taken without knowing their charges and led away from their friends and family for ten to twenty-five years, many of them never coming back. The Soviets would purposely split up families and lovers. If you had a son or a daughter it was virtually guaranteed that you would be put in different camps and have no contact with them. At least when the Soviets committed mass murder, it wasn't based on ethnicity.

Nazi Germany: 16,315,000 victims overall from their concentration camps.

(Rummel, 2020)

The Nazis committed an unprecedented genocide of the Jewish people, an ethnic cleansing. When God was replaced with the government, Hitler and the SS placed themselves in his stead, destroying everything and everyone that was contrary to what they believed was pure. When imperfect humans determine the standards of perfection, they will always hurt those they deem reprehensible.

In order for the Nazis to get into power it required a lot of propaganda from the SS. Not only that, in order for their "truths" to be believable to the masses they had to burn all information that contradicted their mission, hence the infamous book burnings. Once all evidence of God's moral standards were destroyed, there were no ethical safeguards in place to keep the Nazis in check and the citizens forced to live in Nazi Germany had to go along with the insane ethical claims that the SS were implementing. When you have a government that takes the place of God, and a group of cultish followers who walk in lockstep with them completely morally unregulated, you end up with Nazi Germany.

Clearly, from the examples above we can draw the conclusion that when the government begins to see itself as the granter of freedoms rather than as a protector of them, authoritarianism is sure to follow. When a government believes it, rather than God, is responsible for granting your freedoms, it takes God's place, always resulting in innocent citizens' loss of freedom, and often in many of their deaths.

When we allow the idea that it is government that grants rights instead of God, we also subconsciously make room for the idea that the government can take our rights away. The mere thought of this being a possibility in America is scary enough, but as I'll discussed in Chapter Five, politicians have no interest in protecting your rights; they see them as something to give and take, not as something to be upheld and protected.

This was made perfectly clear during the Covid-19 lockdowns with online censorship of valid information and a refusal on the part of government to admit basic truths. We've entered a time in which our culture has forgotten that our rights were given to us by God, which has led to our government being filled with bureaucrats who believe they can legislate your rights away. The right to gather? Gone. The right to speak your mind freely? Gone. The right to bear arms? They're working on it. This is real. Our population has been satisfied with the distractions of social media and other media outlets for so long, that we've forgotten how strongly absolute power corrupts.

Freedom and safety are not necessarily mutually exclusive, as there is a certain safety that comes with cultivating skill sets to deal with difficult situations and having confidence in yourself. When you are taken care of by the government, however, that form of "safety" will always clash with your inherent freedoms.

I understand the desire to keep church and state separate. And I agree that personal affiliations between heads of organized religion and political officials constitute a conflict of interest. Having the Church be subject to the state or the state subject to the Church has led to many tragedies throughout history.

However, this does not exclude political leaders from being able to actively attend religious functions or from having personal value structures that place a higher power above them. In fact, in my opinion, having such a value structure would make them much more qualified to be a protector of our rights and freedoms than if they did not. This is because they would understand that our freedom is something to be protected, not granted.

Having a personal relationship with God is one of the most freeing and liberating things you can do in your lifetime. Once you become aware that there is a God, not only will you become conscious of the blessings you already have in your life, you'll be able to actively add to them by entreating God with prayer and manifestation.

Prayer works just like the law of attraction. The difference is that when you pray, you ask God to lend some of his energy to you in the manifestation process, allowing for a more powerful manifestation than we could accomplish on our own. That being the case, when you pray you must focus on the desired outcome, as with the law of attraction. This implies that the best way to pray is to ask for what you desire, not to avoid something you don't want. For example, if you're running late for work in the morning and praying to God you'll make it on time for work, the best prayer would be to ask to arrive on time. What many people do instead is ask not to be late. There is a difference here, however subtle, and it has everything to do with manifestation.

When you say a prayer such as "Please allow me to be on time for work," where's the focus? The focus is "on time for work." There's nothing undesirable in this prayer. Everything is exactly what you need it to be: an attempted manifestation of getting to work on time. In the other example, "Please don't let me be late," the focus is on being late rather than being on time. According to the law of attraction, you get what you focus on, and if you're praying to God to not be late rather than to arrive on time, you're focusing on what you don't want, and manifesting it. This changes the approach for those who want to pray effectively; after all, it's all about your perspective and attitude.

So when you pray, focus on exactly what you want to happen, not on preventing what you don't want. God is *big*, remember? God is capable of blessing you with what you truly want. Praying for something to not happen is like telling someone not to think about something: you'll still manifest it in your life whether you mean to or not. Instead, get really specific about what you do want. The more specific you get, the better the prayer will work.

As I stated in Chapter One, truth is freedom. Without the concept of truth, defined as the property of being in accordance with facts and reality, you cannot have freedom.

Believing in truth, especially moral truth, creates a foundation from which to make good decisions. Without truth, freedom is anarchy. Just as you can't navigate a ship without a compass, you cannot make good decisions without a foundation in reality. Individual freedom implies the power to act, which requires objective truth, without it, you're cast away at sea with no reference point to tell you where you are.

Let's take a look at the New Testament to see how this connects to God.

"Then you will know the truth, and the truth shall set you free" (John 8:32). A common idea across many religions is the concept that God is truth. What does that mean? It means God is perfect and unchanging, and because God created our souls and instilled in them the moral compass discussed in Chapter Three, we have a direct line of access to that truth. Through our spirits, which also motivate us to be free in the first place, we are able to make decisions that enable our freedom and perpetuate it. The only reason this is possible is because God is the pinnacle of truth. Through God, we have been granted a desire to be free and the innate decision-making skills to enable that freedom through our spirits. The concept of natural rights only exists because of the idea that we are all God's children; that is, at our core, we are all divine spiritual beings having a human experience. Without the idea that God grants you your freedoms, they become something that can be traded away.

We've discussed why the existence of a God is paramount to freedom today (because God grants you your natural rights and your desire to be free), but how do psychedelics of all things tie into God and the meaning of life? How does that impact your freedom? The book *The Immortality Key*, by Brian C. Muraresku, has quite a lot to say on the link between these ideas. It is Brian's assertion that

> when it comes to "God"—a word rarely used by the mystics—there is total unanimity on one crucial issue of paramount importance. God does not reside in a holy book.
> (Muraresku, 2020)

In this book, Muraresku explains the origins of psychedelic drugs as best we currently understand it, and goes on to explain the quiet history of psychedelics in the Christian faith. It's no secret that when Moses saw the burning bush he was likely having a DMT (or Dimethyltryptamine) experience. Benny Shanon, a professor at Jerusalem's Hebrew University, believes that Moses was having a psychedelic experience:

> "In the philosophy journal Time and Mind, Benny Shanon states that key events of the Old Testament are actually records of visions by ancient Israelites high on hallucinogens…. Hardly an incident in the

Bible is spared Shanon's drug-focused reading.
Acacia trees, used by Noah to build the ark, were
revered because some varieties contain the
psychedelic substance dimethyltryptamine (DMT)."
(Jeffay, 2008)

You may be surprised to know that psychedelics have a history in Christian traditions as well as ceremonies. Bryan Muraresku, author of *The Immortality Key* Spends the bulk of the 400-page book describing in great detail a psychedelic recipe for wine, and why this wine was so important in the early days of Christianity.

In *The Immortality Key*, Muraresku brings together evidence for a spiked psychedelic wine having been drunk in early church rituals. This implies that there was another component to both religion and spirituality that has been removed by those that came after. Modern spirituality in the West is missing an important component: living the experience for yourself. Muraresku talks about this form attained by spiritual leaders and enlightened ones and called "death before death."

What is death before death? It is a radical change in one's thinking, an opening up of the mind to the energies of the universe around them, and a rebirth for that person into the version of themselves that knows the truth. Death before death is when your ego melts into your true spiritual self, allowing you to be your true self unimpeded.

A few people throughout history have attained this level of connection with God and the collective consciousness around them through years of training and discipline. However, it is very probable that psychedelics were used to aid and speed up this process in early Christianity as well as leading up to it. In regards to psychedelics and consciousness change, Muraresku had this to say:

> I attribute the absolute highest importance to consciousness change. I regard psychedelics as catalyzers for this. They are tools which are guiding our perception toward other deeper areas of human existence so that we again become aware of our spiritual essence.
> (Muraresku, 2020)

Psychedelics provide you with this experiential component of spirituality. They open your mind, allowing you to actually experience the flow of all things and to truly understand how our energies are all connected on a spiritual level. When they're taken in a safe environment, with a guide (I do not advise unsafe recreational use!), psychedelics have been clinically proven to help people relax into the flow of the afterlife.

Dr. Stephen Ross, an associate professor of psychiatry at NYU Langone Health in New York City, has researched and conducted experiments where psilocybin and LSD is administered to terminal cancer patients. Naturally, physiological and existential distress is common with having a terminal illness, and there was already some promising experimentation done in the 70's with psychedelics and cancer-related terminal distress. Over the last two decades, after years of faux-science, therapy to help with the cancer-related distress using psychedelics has resumed. With a compilation of clinical trials from 1960-2018 on the therapeutic use of psychedelics on patients with terminal illnesses, they found ten clinical trials with four-hundred-forty-five participants, most of which had terminal cancer. It was their findings that of those ten trials, six studies conducted with LSD from 1964-1980 may have improved the patients cancer-related anxiety, depression, and fear of death. Four studies conducted mostly with psilocybin between 2011 and 2016 showed that psychedelic-assisted therapy can produce quick, strong, and sustainable improvements in cancer related existential distress. (Ross, 2018)

Psychedelics, in a controlled environment, have been proven to help ease cancer patients' anxieties and depression related to their illness even in terminal cases. Dr. Ross has talked about another enlightening aspect of psychedelics. In an interview, Ross is quick to point to some of the flaws in the studies he's conducted with cancer patients and psychedelics, including the lack of control variables. He also points out that most of the people in the study were in either full or partial remission, and that it's possible they would've been feeling good without the psilocybin. However, he also highlights that out of the fifteen patients in the study, sixty to eighty percent of them met the parameters for clinically meaningful reductions in their anxiety and depression. That being:

Nearly all...still described their psilocybin experience as one of the most personally or spiritually meaningful ones of their lives.
(Norton, 2020)

So we know that psychedelics ease people's pain when they're faced with the idea of death. But why? The real answer is we don't know, or at least we have no concrete way of knowing at the time of writing.

However, one can speculate and infer that, based on the psychedelic origins of Christianity and the proven fact that psychedelic use is effective in easing people's pain when faced with death, it's a real possibility that they provide humans with a living component of our true spiritual selves, allowing us, for a brief while, to see things on the spiritual plain and truly connect with God on a literal level. Perhaps this eases people's anxiety by showing them a "bigger picture" of the eternities and expanding their perspective.

Something like this, a death before death, is possible without psychedelics. One could spend years training and working to accomplish this level of connection with God and become spiritually attuned enough to reach states like these.

If that's true, one could argue that the training is necessary to appreciate the experience. I would argue that the level of appreciation required for that type of connection to God and the universe is so exceedingly high that it defies the circumstances of how such an incredible experience came about. In fact, there was a John Hopkins study in 2014, in which psychedelics were used to help participants quit smoking, and many of the participants were still extremely appreciative of the experience after. At 6 months into the experiment, 80% (twelve of fifteen) of smokers in the pilot study had abstained from cigarettes for at least 1 week, as confirmed by breathalyzer and urine tests. Typical success rates for abstinence are less than 35%. Johnson and his colleagues found in a follow-up paper that 67% of participants remained smoke-free 12 months after their quit date, and 60% reported to have quit smoking for 6 months or more. Overall, the majority of subjects who took psilocybin felt that the experience was one of the most meaningful and spiritually significant they'd ever had. (Lewis, 2020)

One of the most meaningful experiences in they've

ever had? That would be on the same level as, say, holding your first child for the first time or standing across the altar and getting married. If these experiences are that powerful and improve people's addictive habits this much in clinical studies, I would argue that these substances are at least worth exploring. I would also assert the possibility that they may be the missing link allowing us as humans to truly experience the spiritual plain and connect with the infinite love around us. When you're full of love and positive energy, you automatically want to steer away from things that harm you, such as smoking. On a spiritual level, it makes sense that this is an effective treatment.

Taking this into account with the studies from John Hopkins, it's a safe hypothesis that the psychedelics opened the participants up to being healed at an energetic level by allowing their perceptions to shift. This alteration in perception was the critical shift, what Dr. Sue Morrison in her book titled *The Energy Codes* calls the "quantum shift." Psychedelics opened them up to a realization that they are spiritual beings having a human experience, giving them the death before death that was talked about in *The Immortality Key*.

Sometimes, it's easier to treat the spiritual components of a problem before you treat the physical and mental parts. Remember, the universe and God function on an energetic, spiritual level. Describing a freak physical injury her mother incurred, Dr. Morrison said:

According to the science of bioenergetics, the study of the body's energy field, a "fracture" occurs first in the energy field, and then manifests in the physical world when we step off the curb and break our ankle. We step into what already exists in our subtle energy

body. Something else was going on with my mom, since clearly not everyone who turns to dry her hands breaks a leg! It is possible that the fractured bone was caused by an energetic fracture—a dispersed energy that shot down her leg in order to be grounded. She had a blockage in her field, and it played out in that moment as she turned her leg.
(Morter and Bolte Taylor, 2020, p. 193)

Dr. Morrison's mom had a fracture in her energy field before it manifested physically in her body. Problems and solutions often first manifest energetically, and second physically. This implies that we can solve a lot of our problems through energy rather than physical or mental means. With psychedelics, it is my hypothesis that they allow the energy around a person to be healed, and in the process help heal mental ailments. They do this by providing people with a real tangible experience that connects them to their inner spirit and the spirituality of the world around them, opening them up to the infinite healing powers of the universe.

Whether you call it enlightenment, a quantum shift, death before death, or a mystical experience, all of the evidence points to these substances being an important part of human history and human spirituality. While it is possible to achieve these states without the use of psychedelics, the successful achievement of a quantum shift through them and the positive effect of their use in safe controlled environments are unquestionable.

Why is this so important? Psychedelics can provide you with a true spiritual experience that so many of us lack, a living experience that allows you to truly understand the flow of the energies around you and your connection with God on a literal level. Once you are awakened to how you are

107

literally connected with God and everything else around you, it not only becomes impossible to deny God's existence, it also becomes very painful to participate in low-vibrational actions. Psychedelics have not been proven to be addictive, despite how effective they are at treating these illnesses. This is a promising sign that psychedelic abuse is much less likely than abuse of other drugs.

When you feel the love vibrating inside of you on a spiritual level, and you feel your connection with God and your true spiritual self rather than the ego, you enable yourself to seek true freedom. In those moments, when you are open to all of the love and positivity around you, allowing you to love unimpededly and receive love unimpededly, and feel truly connected to God, your spirit will be the freest it can be while tethered to your body during this life.

Even if you're imprisoned physically or mentally, your spirit can still attain this sense of liberation and freedom through training, prayer, a connection with God, and perspective-changing events. The spirit is the ultimate healer, and by cultivating a relationship with God through the spirit, we are able to heal all of the toxicity that we accumulate in our earthly lives.

Keep in mind that change is hard, and a shattering of the ego is not always a pleasant experience. It can be difficult and very humbling to learn just how small you are on a literal level. However, if you stay open to love and connect to God, you will replace your fragile, shattered ego with your resilient, true spiritual self and live the most spiritually free life you can, feeling immense satisfaction from the love generated.

We've covered why God is integral to our freedoms, and we've just covered how psychedelics are useful tools to aid in your attaining spiritual freedom. Now, in this last section of the chapter, we're going to cover how this is connected to the inherent meaning of human existence. Of course, this is just my theory, but I truly believe that the purpose of human experience is to allow us to live a life free to pursue joy. Looking at several ancient holy texts from several different religions, the similarities in their themes are impossible to ignore. When referring to humankind's purpose, God always outlines the importance of having Joy in our hearts.

Absolutely, GOD's allies have nothing to fear, nor will they grieve.
They are those who believe and lead a righteous life.
For them, joy and happiness in this world, as well as in the Hereafter.
(Qur'an, 10:62–10:64)

Adam fell that men might be; and men are, that they might have joy.
(Smith, 1981, Nephi 2:25)

The prospect of the righteous is joy, but the hopes of the wicked come to nothing.
(*King James Bible*, Proverbs 10:28)

Seven days you shall celebrate a feast to the LORD your God in the place which the LORD chooses, because the LORD your God will bless you in all your produce and in all the work of your hands, so that you will be altogether joyful.
(Deuteronomy 16:15, NASB)

There is no path to happiness: happiness is the path.
(Gautama Buddha)

No matter what belief system you choose to adopt, what they all have in common is that if you believe in a higher power, such as God or source energy, you desire to live a free life in pursuit of joy. But why? Because, in my humble opinion, the meaning of life is to live a free, full of joy and connectedness to God and those around you.

To live is to be free. At our core, Humans desire freedom more than anything else. We, the humans of the world, feel it is our birthright to live freely, especially when we are young. It is conditioning by a culture of captivity that teaches subservience. Freedom comes naturally, captivity is taught.

No one knows this truth more than mothers. Mothers, who must discipline their children from wild beasts into civilized persons, know the difficulty of teaching humans to quell their innate desire to explore and express themselves completely uninhibited. Children, at their core, feel a desire to be free that far exceeds their desire to listen to the rules.

It is only when their parents (most often mothers, statistically) discipline them that they learn the consequences of making poor decisions. You may have free agency, but you don't get to decide the natural consequences of your actions, and most children have yet to develop a sense of cause and effect. This means that by making mistakes, they are able to learn which actions lead to positive consequences and which lead to negative ones. One could argue that the freedom to make mistakes is universally essential to growth and learning and fundamental for our own development as adults, not just as children.

At our core, we desire to be free at a spiritual level from negativity. We desire to be free on a mental and physical level from our bad habits and negative thought loops. At an emotional level, we desire the freedom to express ourselves and to pursue and work towards goals. Humans, at a fundamental level, are free creatures. It is our desire to live a free lives in pursuit of joy that elevates our spirits.

The time has come to stop the elevation of weakness and captivity in our culture. If we continue to propagate a culture of captivity, we will lose the freedom that enabled it in the first place. The elected officials in office, along with the FDA and other regulatory agencies (More on that in Chapter 5), don't value your freedom. They see you as a commodity, a thing to be traded. The reason this country was so good in the first place was because its citizens were tough enough to keep the government in line. Our culture of captivity, weakness, anti-responsibility, and anti-work have created an America where freedom is considered "unpopular."

How can freedom be unpopular when your heart and soul yearn to be free every waking moment of every day? Truly those who believe freedom is unpopular have never been in forced captivity with their freedoms stripped from them. Freedom is the one desire that unites every human across the planet.

Let not any one pacify his conscience by the delusion that he can do no harm if he takes no part, and forms no opinion. Bad men need nothing more to compass their ends, than that good men should look on and do nothing. He is not a good man who, without a protest, allows wrong to be committed in his name, and with the means which he helps to supply, because he will not trouble himself to use his mind on the subject. (Mill, 1859)

To deny the forces inside of you pushing for freedom is akin to doing nothing in the face of evil. Too many times throughout the last century we have seen the atrocity of good men looking on and doing nothing. If we do not exercise our freedoms to fix what we already have in front of us, we will all surely perish under totalitarianism.

Everything starts with responsibility and accountability. Fix your immediate area, build yourself up, and work on yourself. Then start to take stewardship of your surroundings, lifting the world up to where you stand. As you help people, more and more will join you in lifting where they stand. Energy has momentum just like everything else. If we can gather enough positive momentum behind responsibility and freedom by teaching self-reliance and accountability, we can save our culture and thus our future.

Freedom is the key to success, joy, and fulfillment in your life. To truly have joy is to be truly free. To truly be free, you must be self-reliant. No one who depends on someone else for their wellbeing can live a free life; it is only when you take responsibility for your own existence and stand on your own two feet that freedom becomes a possibility.

Ultimately, man should not ask what the meaning of his life is, but rather must recognize that it is he who is asked. In a word, each man is questioned by life; and he can only answer to life by answering for his own life; to life he can only respond by being responsible.

(Frankl, 2017)

The time has come for us to return to the old traditions of responsibility, personal accountability, hard work, financial literacy, strong spirituality, and a deep rooting of our lives in freedom. It's time to make freedom mainstream again. Life is all about having the freedom to pursue happiness. As Les Brown put it,

If you can't be happy, what else is there?
(Brown, 2008)

The meaning of life is to live freely in pursuit of joy. Psychedelics, in a safe, controlled setting, combined with a close relationship with God, are vital tools that can help you attain that way of life. Embrace God. Embrace the quantum shift. Embrace joy. Embrace freedom.

Chapter 5: Politics

> Suppose you were an idiot, and suppose you were a
> member of Congress; but I repeat myself.
> (Mark Twain, 1906)

Our freedom is under attack in America, and our politicians
are some of those responsible. This goes without saying, but
I'll say it anyway: politics is a touchy subject, especially at
the moment. The constant demonization and propaganda on
both sides of the political aisle is nauseating, repugnant, and
is killing our freedom. As it stands, political labels mean very
little these days, despite the massive emphasis placed on
them by those in opposing tribes and the media propping
them up. In our culture today, any opinion in the political
sphere is considered polarizing and worth demonizing you
for regardless of your original intent.
Both political parties' elected officials actively
collaborate against the American people's freedoms and best

interests every day so they can stuff their pockets with dirty lobbyist money or receive cushy private sector jobs once their prestigious time in the political limelight comes to a close. This is well known by the vast majority of American people, and yet we continue to ignore the growing issues in Washington like they're no big deal, going about our merry way with skips in our steps and smiles on our faces. No longer can we afford to sit ideally by and allow them to strip us of our freedoms.

Over the course of 2021, America had a discussion that horrified many of its citizens: Do we mandate that companies or the government can force you to take the Covid-19 vaccine in order to gain an income? In this case, companies could fire you for refusing to take the Covid-19 vaccine and the government could require you to take the vaccine in order to shop at a local grocery store, effectively forcing you to take the vaccine just to live in society. Can these giant pharmaceutical companies and the government force you to undergo a private medical procedure? The core question this boils down to is: Do you have the right to *know* and *choose* what goes into your body, otherwise known as bodily autonomy?

Of course, if you believe rights are inalienable and given by God rather than the government, the answer is an unequivocal yes. But as far as legislation is concerned, this is a problem that goes all the way back to the wording of the US Constitution and how it's interpreted. According to Law.Justia.com:

The U.S Constitution safeguards the rights of Americans to privacy and personal autonomy. Although the Constitution does not explicitly provide for such rights, the U.S. Supreme Court has interpreted the Constitution protects these rights, specifically in the areas of marriage, procreation, abortion, private consensual homosexual activity, and medical treatment.

(Justia, 2018)

As you can see, the concept of forced vaccination isn't something that the founders of the nation took into consideration, as the technology and culture of the time were nowhere near where they are today. We as a country need to have this conversation about bodily autonomy. Some people's sense of entitlement has grown so extreme that they truly believe they can force others to undergo a private medical procedure for their own "safety" and "protection." Just as importantly, we need to put laws in place and better enforce existing laws so that these massive pharmaceutical companies have to follow stricter guidelines in regards to what we ingest. And this doesn't only apply to vaccines from pharmaceutical companies.

This fight goes back to when corporations challenged Food and Drug Administration (FDA) regulations requiring them to report their use of food additives. Back in 1958, the FDA passed a rule called the GRAS provision that allowed industry scientists to decide whether an additive is safe to consume, thus effectively bypassing the testing requirements.

The FDA is responsible for overseeing 80% of the food consumed in the United States. That means that 80% of what we have available to eat is allegedly supposed to pass certain requirements and tests to be safe for consumption. The other 20% is still available for purchase, but because those products haven't been FDA approved, the manufacturers of those products can't claim FDA approval on their advertising and thus may not sell as much of their product. Getting FDA approval for a product requires passing rigorous standards and can involve years of red tape... unless you're using additives that are considered generally safe by industry studies. As the FDA themselves specify,

> any substance that is reasonably expected to become a component of food is a food additive that is subject to premarket approval by FDA, unless the substance is generally recognized as safe (GRAS) among experts qualified by scientific training and experience to evaluate its safety under the conditions of its intended use, or meets one of the other exclusions from the food additive definition in section 201(s) of the Federal Food, Drug, and Cosmetic Act (FFDCA). (FDA, 2018)

The problem with this is that the FDA doesn't perform a lot of testing on actual products. Simply put, the FDA relies on industry studies to determine the safety of food additives and new medicines. The Alliance for Natural Health, the largest organization in the USA working to promote and protect natural approaches to regenerating health, have the following to say about the tactics the FDA uses to approve products:

> The FDA uses industry studies to determine if new drugs can come to market. No independent testing is done to check the industry's results. This system presents many opportunities for manipulation. In the past, drug companies have withheld evidence that might lead a drug to be rejected, and the results have been disastrous (see, for example, the approval of Vioxx, which then killed 60,000 people).

(Health, 2016)

Having industry scientists be the ones responsible for deciding whether something is safe to use can lead to conflicts of interest. Industry studies are often bought and paid for by the same large companies that create the products studied in the first place. This creates a dynamic whereby the industry scientists responsible for determining the safety of a new medicine or food additive have a financial incentive to find in favour of the company. As we'll discuss below, large pharmaceutical companies have a history of manipulating results of important studies to their financial benefit. When a corporation is selling mass quantities of food or medicine to the American people, it's unwise to accept their portrayal as benevolent figures: they run a for-profit business just like all of the other big corporations in the world, meaning the only thing they really care about is money. If these big corporations can get away with cutting the costs of production by using cheap ingredients or adding growth hormones, they're going to do it.

The question then becomes: Do these food additives have a negative effect on the human body if consumed every day over a period of years? The answer to that question is a resounding yes. According to an article from the *San Francisco Chronicle*:

Scientists call environmental substances that can potentially alter our bodies' hormone system "endocrine disruptors." Such chemicals – released from manufacturing facilities and commercial products – usually degrade into natural substances. Yet, under some conditions, they stay in the environment and contaminate the food supply. In fact, the authors of a 2017 report in *Genes & Nutrition* concluded that the greatest exposure to endocrine disruptors comes from our diet. Such contamination may affect the basic processes of our bodies. (Meyers, 2018)

Hormone additives in food can also damage your brain and reproductive health. Yet these are considered GRAS or "generally recognized as safe" for use by the FDA and are fast-tracked into a grocery store near you. That's not all either: many consumer goods companies also use partially hydrogenated oil, MSG, high-fructose corn syrup, sodium nitrate, sodium nitrite, BHA, propyl gallate, sodium benzoate, benzoic acid, potassium bromate, and a variety of food colorings, consumption of all of which have been linked to various health problems (Perry, 2016). Yet these companies persist in putting these harmful additives into the food supply without ever having their feet held to the fire.

Possibly most infuriatingly of all, the FDA also has a history of not properly defining important terms related to food. For instance, the FDA had chosen to define the term "natural" as meaning that "nothing artificial or synthetic (including all color additives regardless of source) has been included in, or has been added to, a food that would not normally be expected to be in that food. However, this policy was not intended to address food production methods, such as the use of pesticides" (FDA, 2021)

By refusing to properly adhere to what the word natural truly means, the FDA has enabled gigantic food corporations to label their unhealthy, highly processed products as "natural." Combined with the lack of testing that the FDA does on products because of their reliance on industry studies, which has a direct effect on your freedom to know whether something is safe and healthy to ingest, the FDA has lost the trust of the American people.

We saw this same problem in the FDA's regulation of pharmaceutical companies during the opioid epidemic. The issue may have begun much earlier, but the opioid epidemic is the clearest example we have of corporation's greed overpowering the feeble government agencies put in place to keep them in check.
According to the *AMA Journal of Ethics*, much of the responsibility for creating the opioid crisis lies with the pharmaceutical industry, particularly due to their agressive promotion of prescription opioids. There was even a trial, said to be "the first of its kind," in which the state court of Oklahoma found that the massive increase in opioid addiction, overdose deaths, and babies born exposed to these harmful drugs was directly caused by false advertising and misleading of the medical industry in an attempt to sell more opioids. However, they also make the important assertion that

the fact that opioid manufacturers disseminated false claims regarding the risks and benefits of opioids for the past 25 years points to a dereliction of duty by the US Food and Drug Administration (FDA)—the federal agency charged with regulating pharmaceutical companies.
(Kolodny, 2020)

We have a glaring problem here in the United States. We preach freedom, but our regulatory offices have done very little to protect our freedoms from malpractice by these large companies. Instead, they've been filled to the brim with unelected officials who are never held accountable for giving your freedom away to these large corporations. Pfizer has had to pay 1.195 billion dollars for falsely promoting their four drugs Bextra, Geodon, Zyvox, and Lyrica, claiming that each drug could help with conditions for which they were ill suited. This is *the largest criminal fine ever* imposed by the United States for any matter, and yet not a single person was sent to prison (Rubin, 2009). They falsely advertised that medication could help with certain ailments; people took the medication prescribed by doctors with the intention to do good and either ended up addicted or worse off than before.

This is a case of a regulatory office not functioning properly, and as a result, allowing the checks against corporate oligarchy to crumble. Capitalism, when properly balanced, is usually a good and rewarding endeavour. When capitalism is checked with regulations to prevent corporate oligarchy, it has resulted in the almost complete eradication of extreme poverty here in the USA. There is a claim that's been circulating the internet for years that there are eighteen million people in America living in extreme poverty. However, looking back to just a few years ago before the pandemic hit, there was a study conducted in May of 2019 by the census bureau and the University of Chicago that proved extreme poverty, while present in America, is a statistical anomaly (meaning that it is incredibly rare),

> Specifically analysing $2-a-day poverty—that is, the number of Americans living on $2 or less per day— the study's co-authors found that only 0.11 percent of Americans live in extreme poverty. That comes out to roughly 336,000 people—still too high, but nowhere near 18 million. Moreover, the study concludes that

the extreme poverty rate for parents—whether single or married—is virtually zero."

(Ladan, 2019)

Yet, as we can clearly see with the FDA's lax regulation of large pharmaceutical and food companies, when the checks don't work, are improperly enforced, or are too weak, corporate interests line their pockets at our expense. This issue goes even deeper, however.

Bodily autonomy is a human right, but because the FDA is hampered and ineffective, we have no effective legislation protecting us from these greedy corporate interests filling our food with unsafe additives and marketing addictive pain medicine as being safe for everyday use. If we truly have the right to know what goes into our body, we have to be properly informed about the ingredients in what we eat and how dangerous our medication is. Once we have the facts, it's our choice whether or not to consume these products, but we must have access to that information in order to make an informed decision. This principle is called "informed consent." Informed consent occurs when there is an agreement between parties to render either an action or interaction between them, with both parties aware of all important and relevant facts. This includes the disclosing of all of the risks involved and any possible alternatives. It is only through informed consent that we can truly make any good decisions and live a free life (recall from Chapter One that truth is freedom, and that freedom cannot exist or sustain itself without truth).

Conversely, it's the job of these regulatory agencies to prevent harmful additives from being added to the food and medicine supply in the first place.

As a tax-paying citizen with elected officials, you might expect that the money you pay into the system would have some sort of positive effect on your life, and on rare occasions it does. But when you take into account that the FDA had 18,000 employees as of 2022 and spent 6.5 billion taxpayer dollars a year as of 2018 (FDA, 2018), the effectiveness of the organization as a whole is called into question. After all, none of these 18,000 employees, whose job it is to decide what is safe to go into your food and medicine, are elected. And remember, the US Constitution doesn't explicitly say you have the right to bodily autonomy with regard to medical procedures; this stems from the interpretation the US supreme court, who also hold that you have the right to know what you are ingesting according to the principle of informed consent.

When you choose to do something, you have the right to know the risks involved. Whether it's aggressive opioid prescribing, harmful additives being put into the nation's food supply, or the federal mandating of a new and experimental vaccine with unknown side effects, you have the right to know how something that is certified by the FDA is going to affect your body.

The waters get even darker when we look at medical experimentation. Believe it or not, there is actually a code of ethics that scientists are supposed to follow when they conduct their research. This was settled at the Nuremberg trials after WWII, when Nazi Germany was being held accountable for their many war crimes and crimes against humanity. The set of principles established by the court were titled the Nuremberg Code. They are:

1. Voluntary consent is essential.
2. The results of any experiment must be for the greater good of society.

3. Human experiments should be based on previous animal experimentation.
4. Experiments should be conducted by avoiding physical/mental suffering and injury.
5. No experiments should be conducted if it is believed to cause death/disability.
6. The risks should never exceed the benefits.
7. Adequate facilities should be used to protect subjects.
8. Experiments should be conducted only by qualified scientists.
9. Subjects should be able to end their participation at any time.
10. The scientist in charge must be prepared to terminate the experiment when injury, disability, or death is likely to occur.

Applying this code to a forced-vaccination program begun without any long-term or publicly available data on said vaccination, we see a direct violation of principles 1, 2, 4, 6, 9, and 10. How can you voluntarily consent to something that is forced upon you? How can it be for the greater good of human society when you're forced out of employment for choosing to remain unvaccinated? How can you avoid physical and mental suffering when you lose the right to choose what you put into your own body, essentially losing sovereignty over yourself? How can the benefits outweigh the risks when there is no long-term data on how this will affect people? How can we end our participation if the inoculation is updated every year and you're forced to get vaccinated with each new update? How can you terminate the procedure if millions of people around the world have already been forced to get vaccinated?

These mandates clearly violate the right to bodily autonomy as well as the right to be informed about what it is you're ingesting. I am vehemently against any sort of forced inoculation. To force someone to undergo a private medical procedure and in order to be able to get any sort of income or to buy food is a massive violation of HIPAA (the Health Insurance Portability and Accountability Act), which guarantees your right to medical privacy.

The HIPAA Privacy Rule establishes national standards to protect individuals' medical records and other individually identifiable health information (collectively defined as "protected health information") and applies to health plans, health care clearinghouses, and those health care providers that conduct certain health care transactions electronically. The Rule requires appropriate safeguards to protect the privacy of protected health information and sets limits and conditions on the uses and disclosures that may be made of such information without an individual's authorization
(U.S. Department of Health & Human Services, 2015)

You have the right to choose whom you disclose your medical information to, and you certainly have the right to confidentiality in the doctor's office. The government's forcing of a vaccine passport/mandate onto the citizens of the United States is a massive violation of your HIPAA rights. Nowadays, it's everyone's business if you've undergone a private medical procedure, that is, if you've gotten vaccinated. The most commonly used argument is that you have to do it for the good of the whole community. However, given what we've learned about the FDA's lax regulation of these large pharmaceutical companies, and because the vaccines were rushed through the authorization process due to an emergency declaration, it is a fair argument to say that these corporations do not have your best interest at heart and neither does the FDA. Forced vaccination is against the interest of the American people.

Since their inception, some of the Covid-19 vaccines have been officially approved by the FDA, though it's questionable what this means given their standards of approval. Looking back to Chapter One, we learned that the brain has neuroplasticity, meaning that over time and with repetition, habits become easier to follow. If over the last fifty-seven years the FDA and these large corporations have been getting away with lying to you about how safe their products are, it's safe to say that they're still lying today about the products they currently release and approve. It's also a safe bet that the American people have been listening to these lies for so long that they've grown to believe them.

Some citizens of this country truly believe that these organizations are benevolent forces, when it's plain to see the opposite is true.

This being the case, it is ethically and morally wrong to impose a mandate forcing free citizens of this country to get vaccinated just to earn an income or shop at a grocery store. You have the right to life, liberty, and the pursuit of happiness, and the imposition of a forced-vaccination program detracts from those rights.

You have the God-given right to choose what goes into your body, and the government, your workplace, and the Centers for Disease Control have no right to take that away from you. On a moral level, it is wrong to force a vaccine mandate onto every citizen of the country just because some people don't feel safe after getting vaccinated. Personal accountability means that you have to take responsibility for your *own* existence, not other people's.

However, on the topic of health, our culture seems to have adopted a group mentality rather than an individualistic one. Instead of taking personal responsibility for your health by doing things like exercising, eating right, and taking care of yourself, now you're considered healthy if you're affirmed by everyone in the group.

If the political tribe or pop-culture opinion group you subscribe to arbitrarily decides that you're unhealthy whether due to an unpopular opinion, a lifestyle choice, or a personal belief, you're ostracized and forced into submission by online "keyboard warriors" regardless of your stance. "Keyboard warrior" is a term for people who fight for social-justice-related issues online by shaming, insulting, or doxing those they disagree with. If none of those options work, these so-called warriors will proceed to attempt to ruin your reputation, have you fired from your job, or create enough outrage to have you permanently removed from social media sites. The rabble on both sides of the political spectrum can easily be observed by simply scrolling through your social media feed. A perfect example of this was when the "Libs of TikTok" account got suspended for doing nothing more than reposting what other users of the website post (as the name suggests, those of the liberal persuasion) and pointing out their hypocrisy. Yet they were suspended on April 13th, 2022, because of the outrage from keyboard warriors.

However, if you follow the group's health narrative, whatever it may be at a given moment, you're rewarded with validation to the highest degree, even if the prescribed behaviours are actually unhealthy.

Not only are there legitimate medical reasons for people to remain unvaccinated, there are also legitimate concerns about the efficacy and immediate and long-term side effects of this inoculation. Necessarily, there are no ten-year studies of any of the Covid-19 vaccines. We have no idea what the long-term effects of this mRNA vaccine will be on the population. These are legitimate concerns that people should be allowed to have.

Over the last year, we've seen countless people demonized for not being pro-vaccine enough. Suddenly, if you question one vaccine you're deemed an anti-vaxxer and a science denier. Robert Malone, a man whose work, along with that of many other scientists, led to the creation of mRNA technology, was smeared relentlessly for being on Joe Rogan's podcast and stating his professional opinion on the technology. Dr. Malone is more than qualified to speak on these matters:

Dr. Malone is the inventor of mRNA vaccines. The initial patent disclosures for RNA and DNA vaccination were written by Dr. Malone in 1988-1989. Dr. Malone was also an inventor of DNA vaccines in 1988 and 1989. He wrote the patent disclosures and helped design the initial experiments, which were carried out by Dr. Gary Rhodes - in consultation with Dr. Malone... From US PATENT #US6867195B1

(Malone, n.d.)

He literally owns the patent and created the technology, yet he's not considered an authoritative source. This state of affairs is the result of another one of our political freedoms coming under attack: freedom of speech.

One of the biggest issues up for debate in our culture as of writing, one which has a massive impact on freedom of speech in the US, is the fact that corporate interests have zero accountability for silencing people's voices. This is the controversial topic of section 230.

Section 230 of Title 47 of the United States Communications Decency Act was originally written and put into law in 1996, when the internet was still well in its infancy compared to today. The law, specifically Section 2 a+b states:

No provider or user of an interactive computer service shall be held liable on account
Of—
(A) any action voluntarily taken in good faith to restrict access to or availability of material that the provider or user considers to be obscene, lewd, lascivious, filthy, excessively violent, harassing, or otherwise objectionable, whether or not such material is constitutionally protected; or
(B) any action taken to enable or make available to information content providers or others the technical means to restrict access to material described in paragraph (1).
(United States Code, 2006 Edition, Supplement 5, Title 47)

At first glance, nothing seems wrong here. But upon further inspection, the poor wording of the bill is impossible to ignore. The wording in section A, specifically "Any action taken in good faith to restrict access" and "Whether or not such material is constitutionally protected," means that tech companies can remove people they disagree with from their platforms as long as they're labelled "objectionable," or in more modern terms, hateful, racist, homophobic, bigoted, fascist, or misogynistic. If you are removed from a social media platform, the company in question doesn't have to *prove* that what you said was objectionable. Under the protection offered by Section 230, all they have to do is change the public perception of what was said, *framing* it as objectionable, even if it's factual.

(It should go without saying that if you're racist or hateful, you're a terrible person; you're definitely not connected to your inner spirit or the world around you, and you have serious issues that you need to work on. Being racist or hateful in any way is never ok, and I'm not condoning it.)

It's no secret that the vast majority of news media in the US is left-leaning. This bias affects their framing and portrayal of their subject matter (the news). When this happens, opinions sneak their way into the public discourse disguised as facts.

Sources like Wikipedia will then go on to record these opinion pieces as fact, often without first offering their subjects any opportunity to correct the record. After all, Wikipedia is edited by a community of people, and some people are bound to also share this left-leaning bias. Once these entries into Wikipedia are completed, they're officially canon in the factual universe of the internet.

Under section 230, we've enabled social media platforms to remove anyone the group of keyboard warriors and "social activists" has decided isn't virtuous enough: they can "factually" prove that a given statement is objectionable, as they now have a news article and a Wikipedia entry to back up their claim. This despite the fact that both pieces of "evidence" could be completely fabricated.

All that these media and big tech companies have to do if they don't like what you have to say is follow the same method to silence your voice. It'll start with smears on social media, then progress to a news article or opinion piece about the manufactured outrage, after which it's considered a fact on Wikipedia and fact-checkers make the rounds on the internet defaming your character. Once that's done, they can suspend or ban your account for "violating our terms of service," "spreading misinformation" or "objectionable content."

To be fair, there is a legitimate argument to be made from a libertarian perspective in favour of this state of affairs. After all, if you don't like it you can just go build your own social media company, right? Except, all of the new social media companies that have popped up since the big trio took power (Alphabet's Google, Twitter, and Meta) have been acquired by either one of those three or a company that belongs to them. That, or they mysteriously lose the ability to put their apps on the Play Store and Apple App Store, where a combined 5.7 million apps are available.

This rule isn't ironclad, however, as there are alternative social media platforms out there, such as Minds.com, Gab, and Gettr. Still, although it is encouraging to see open resistance to the power that these big tech companies wield, there needs to be a change in the wording of Section 230. Its original intention, to protect the users of the internet, has backfired, allowing for censorship of information and the silencing of important discourse online.

In order to make a change towards freedom of speech and expression, we need to change the way we view these platforms. We should consider them public platforms instead of editorial ones. The internet is the new town square. This was made extremely apparent during the Covid-19 quarantines, when everyone was forced to lockdown and communicate through technology rather than in person. The fact that you can be silenced on these social media platforms for having unpopular opinions clearly means that they are private editorial platforms, and not the open public platforms they claim to be.

If social media platforms are curating content and choosing what goes viral, what people see, what you're allowed to upload, and the opinions you're allowed to voice on their platforms, and if they can remove you if you don't comply, they are wielding the power of an editor, such as at the *New York Times* or the *Wall Street Journal*, a power not conducive to running an open platform.

At these editorial news agencies, the executives have the final say regarding what goes into their papers' stories, what gets published, and what information they reluctantly decide to throw your way. They edit the information, and then they present it to you. However, we know that's the case when we use their services. All of us are well aware of the fact that every news outlet has a certain bias, and that isn't necessarily a bad thing as long as journalistic integrity still exists (which for the most part it doesn't).

Through the rise of the internet and automatic fact-checking, one can easily pull up genuine information alongside the news broadcasts in real time and see quite alarmingly that much of what is told to the American people to be fact is actually a fabrication. My favourite example of this is the Jussie Smollett saga. Jussie Smollett is an actor who starred on a show called *Empire*. On January 29th, 2019, Smollet made a report to the police in alleging that he had been a victim of a hate crime in Chicago. He claimed that two masked assailants poured an unknown substance onto him, presumed to be bleach, and wrapped a rope around his neck. The assailants proceeded to shout homophobic slurs towards him and yell political slogans like "MAGA

Country." Once the police had identified the people of interest, it was discovered that the pair of alleged assailants and Mr. Smollett had a relationship. Both assailants were released after speaking to the police and explaining that they had actually helped Smollett concoct the hate crime to gain publicity. Smollett was later charged with felony disorderly conduct, turned himself into the police, and after a year of going back and forth on the charges, was eventually charged with five out of six counts of filing a false police report related to the attack. (Francescani, 2019)

With all that information in mind, look back and watch to see how most news agencies covered the Jussie Smollett story. You'll begin to notice a disturbing trend. These new agencies all refused to give air-time to the idea, (even after the investigation and during the trial) that he was guilty. It was only after their narrative collapsed, and a guilty verdict was delivered that these media companies like CNN began to change their tune; these massive news corporations are too invested in controlling the narrative to be objective in their reporting.

The difference between news outlets and social media platforms is that social media platforms claim to apply platform rules without bias and to censor content according to their guidelines, meaning that these companies deny having any implicit bias against certain groups. An implicit bias is a preconception attributing specific qualities to a particular group of people. In some cases these policies work, as they can be used to keep age-restricted content, such as pornography or extreme violence, off of platforms where they would be inappropriate. But in most cases they result in progressive social media companies reacting punitively to those they disagree with, while those in their tribe get away with obscenities.

If the social media companies apply their terms of service to even a single person, they must be applied equally to everyone on their platform. Partisan favoritism must stop if we are ever going to move forward as a country.

One of the best attributes of life in the United States is that you have the freedom to say whatever you'd like, short of credible rape and death threats. Basically, you can't call people to violence or threaten violence against others. Everything else is fair game. Keep in mind that while you may have the right to say whatever you want, you don't have the right to choose how others react to it. Kindness and respect are the best policies, especially if you don't know the person you're interacting with.

That being said, there is another cultural problem that has reared its head politically over the last five years, and that is the teaching of young people to interpret words they don't like as violence. This creates a disconnect between those who desire to be disagreeable and those who are pro-conformity.

There will always be disagreeable people in the world, and up until this point in our culture, we'd accepted that. In the past, we taught our children to be resilient to speech-related adversity. Nowadays, you'll seldom hear "Sticks and stones may break my bones, but words will never hurt me" on a playground.

Before the shift towards seeing words as violent, people with disagreeing viewpoints could discuss things of a sensitive nature, such as politics, religion, and personal opinions, without feeling attacked or demonized by each other. People may not have seen eye to eye on certain topics, but they could still sit down and talk about it together and perhaps come to some sort of reconciliation whereby both parties could coexist happily.

After this shift, however, whenever someone gets offended during challenging discourse, they act as though they've been physically assaulted, relentlessly and defensively smearing the other person as a deplorable human. This gross overreaction is part of a broader toxic political habit that the West has been supporting for much too long. As Dave Chappelle put it: "It's too hard to entertain a country whose ears are so brittle. Motherf**kers are so sensitive." (Chappelle, 2017)

There are several problems with this form of reactionary living. The first is that humans are complex, polymorphic creatures. People have depth. As a fundamental survival trait, humans had to learn to perform multiple tasks extremely well, such as gathering or hunting for food, farming, innovating technology, and engaging in warfare, to name a few. Because of these traits, we as human beings are polymorphic by nature, meaning that we can be more than one thing.

When we get offended, we tend to put people into a box that categorizes them in terms of how they've offended us. When we do this, we dehumanize them by taking away their innate human capacity to be more than one thing. In our mind, they're just a terrible person. A stain. An other. When in reality they're human beings just like us. In order to see people we vehemently disagree with as humans rather than as obstacles, we must remember that we are all connected on a spiritual level and apply this principle to our interactions with others.

Obviously, there are reasonable times at which to be offended. I'm not saying that you should never be upset when treated unfairly. However, the culture in America over the last twenty years has taught its young people that it is socially acceptable to have hate in your heart for your fellow

Americans if they disagree with you. This line of thinking essentially dehumanizes them in your mind. This deepens the political and social divide even further, and sets up the next generation to be more polarized than we are already. When you allow yourself to see those with opposing views as less than human, you unconsciously decide that your treatment of them will be subhuman, and if you devalue them to the point that you actively despise them for their beliefs, you may contribute to low-vibrational dialogues that do more to negatively impact the issues at hand than help solve them. If you allow yourself to actively hate others for a difference of opinion, you will actively seek to rob them of their freedoms. Where has this shift in our culture come from?

"A culture that allows the concept of "safety" to creep so far that it equates emotional discomfort with physical danger is a culture that encourages people to systematically protect one another from the very experiences embedded in daily life that they need in order to become strong and healthy.
(Lukianoff and Haidt, 2019)

In *The Coddling of the American Mind*, Greg Lukianoff and Jonathan Haidt explore the reasons why colleges have begun banning speakers who may be considered disagreeable and how this ties into concepts like helicopter parenting and teaching children that they're fragile. Considering that both authors are rather moderate, the book provides a great objective look at why our children are becoming too sensitive to handle the smallest of adversities or to have conversations in which they may be subjected to ideas they disagree with. The authors mention three "untruths" at the beginning of their book that are actively being taught to students in colleges today: "What doesn't kill you makes you weaker," "Always trust your feelings," and "Life is a battle between good people and evil people."

Looking at these untruths, it's clear how they could be harmful to a developing human. Teaching students that they are weak through the maxim "What doesn't kill you makes you weaker" detracts from the resilience that all humans have. On top of this, it makes discourse about complex issues impossible, as it's uncomfortable to have difficult discussions. When you equate words that make you uncomfortable with acts of violence, you take away freedom of speech for your own safety of opinion. Teaching students to avoid things that are difficult will only result in their being unwilling to challenge the popular narrative and go against the grain, to challenge themselves and grow. They will seek to be comfortable rather than successful, and they won't know how to handle the inevitable confrontations inherent to the real world.

Telling students to "always trust their feelings" is highly illogical, as it teaches them to always believe that what they feel is correct, and to distrust anyone who feels differently. This subtracts any nuance from conversation and removes the possibility that one could ever be wrong about something in their mind, making learning impossible, as we are all wrong at some point. Even worse, this untruth can be used to teach that objective reality is less important than a reality that is felt to exist, removing students from the real world at an intellectual level. This makes people easy to control on a massive scale, because if you are not living in reality, you're not able to properly interpret facts, meaning that it's much easier to lie to you.

The final untruth, "Life is a battle between good people and evil people," is especially dangerous when combined with the other two. If you're taught to always trust your feelings and that being challenged intellectually is physically dangerous, when you eventually come across people that disagree with you, you'll instantly dehumanize them. If you believe life is a battle between good and evil people, and you always trust your feelings, then if you believe you are a good person you'll give yourself moral justification to do terrible things in the name of good. And if you believe you are a bad person, you'll feel no guilt or hesitancy to do bad things, because you already believe yourself to be immoral.

When these dangerous untruths are applied at the political level, we see mass unrest and the division of people through their politics. Thus, the best way to uphold the freedom and societal fabric of this country is through civil discourse in the public square, whether this be online or in person, and by allowing yourself to be ok with differences of opinion.

One of the reasons this has become such a problem is due to people's lack of personal responsibility for the way they react to things they don't like. In our toxic culture you're totally justified in screaming at that old lady or berating that guy walking down the street if it's for what's perceived to be a righteous cause. After all, you believe the untruth that the world is made up of good people battling evil people. When you face no social ramifications for immature outbursts, your brain remembers this for next time, and it gives you the green light to freak out whenever you come across something that triggers those emotions. Not only that, everyone in your group will begin to see this as acceptable behavior.

Over time, people learn how to dehumanize those they perceive as their opposition. Eventually, people just see an opposing tribe. If someone you perceive as bad gets upset at your outburst against them, that's just more fuel to add to your supposedly righteous fire. After all, you're the benevolent one, right? It's your job to tell people how to live and why they're wrong. But you're just as human as everyone else, regardless of your political leaning. There's a lot of nuance on the global stage. We live in a world with eight billion people, each of them with their own experiences, backgrounds, and hardships. At what point do you take a step back and say, "Alright, I don't know everything. Let's work on this together."

When your mind is clouded with tribal hate, it's impossible to maintain a cool, calm approach to interactions. When you're overcome by hatred, you subconsciously decide that being right is more important than solving issues that are affecting millions of people. The only way out of the political hellscape we've created is together, united as a country, not divided by political ideology and tribalist leaders.

When a group goes around silencing and belittling those with different opinions for too long, they create an echo chamber of ideas taking in everyone they agree with, making civil discourse even more difficult. In order to combat this trend and remain intellectually free, it's a good idea to have friends on both sides of the political aisle.

This is easier said than done. According to studies conducted by Pew Research, divisions along political lines have widened substantially over the last twenty years, whereas other forms of division have become much less pronounced, meaning that we as a country are becoming hyperpolarized.

The effect of this is even starker when we look at how friendship is divided among party lines.

Overall, 57% of those who identify as Republicans say a lot of their close friends are also Republicans, while another 21% say some of them are. An even larger share of Democrats (67%) say a lot of their close friends are Democrats; an additional 18% say some of their close friends are members of their own party.
(Pew Research Center, 2016)

In comparison, far fewer of those who identify as partisan claim to have friends in the opposing party. Around four-in-ten republicans say they have a lot of friends who are democrats, and about 55% of republicans claim to have a few or no democrat friends. Only 31% of democrats claim to have some republican friends, and 64% of democrats claim to have no republican friends.

According to the same set of data, it was discovered that only 7% of republicans and 6% of democrats had "a lot" of friends in the opposite party. This is a strong sign that we as a country are veering too much into hyperpolarization.

In many case throughout history, hyperpolarization has led to civil war. The best way to liberate and free yourself from the political divide is to stop dehumanizing those on the other side of the political aisle. This is accomplished by cultivating friendships with people who may disagree with you. Politics isn't the only subject to talk about. People are polymorphic, remember? There are many other topics of conversation that are just as important as politics and which need to be discussed.

This is most evident in independent, non-partisan people. Those who aren't associated with a political party are much more likely to be friends with people on either side of the traditional political divide. They express virtually no bias one way or the other, except that they display a preference for being around other independents rather than partisans. This very well may be because of the negativity associated with partisan fighting.

Friendship is one of the only ways to heal the political divide in this country. By thinking of people you disagree with as actual humans rather than as the opposition, you enable a connection with them to develop and allow for civil discourse in order to reach a consensus. It's time to bring humanity back to the political conversation. For all of the talk of human rights on both sides of the political spectrum, no one seems to view the opposing party as actual human beings, making the peaceful negotiation of policy virtually impossible. In order to have real conversations, both parties must act in good faith. It is imperative that both parties involved actively work to fix the problem rather than earning social points for being right. If we can humanize our political discourse, we can remain free, with the liberties we have been blessed with in this great country. If we do not, we will almost certainly be led into captivity by the government.

You have the right to be objectionable, unpopular, and disagreeable. You don't have the right to hurt or threaten to hurt others. This may seem counterintuitive to some people: as we discussed before, our colleges have been teaching the next generation that words can be considered violence. When you take away people's right to be disagreeable and unpopular, you take away their freedom of thought. Those arguing for censorship will claim that being objectionable is the same as being violent, hence the perceived backwardness of my previous statement. However, as Johnathan Haidt discovered, resilience to speech-related adversity is how we as humans grow and learn, falsifying the idea that challenging and even obscene speech can be considered violence. When the definition of what is acceptable behavior keeps changing, it is important to remember that you have the right to act however you like and live however you'd like only as long as you're not bringing harm to another person or encroaching on their rights.

A perfect example of this in American history is the prohibition of alcohol. From 1920 to 1933 in the United States, you were not allowed to buy or sell alcohol. Drinking was considered taboo and immoral behavior. However, the law alone, and even combined with the societal consequences of getting caught drinking, did very little to stop people from imbibing. Illegal bars and breweries started to pop up all over the country, with law enforcement very unmotivated to do anything about it. After all, the cops were human too, and a good percentage of them probably frequented the bars they were supposed to be shutting down. The failure of Prohibition proved that people will continue doing something even if it's looked down upon or made illegal.

The same rule could be applied to the debate we face today between freedom of speech and politeness. If you remove people's right to be objectionable, they won't stop doing the things you find unacceptable. Instead, what will more likely be the case is that you'll create two echo chambers, one of which will belong to you and all of your benevolent friends, the other to those you consider obscene and disagree with. Eventually, the echoes in each group will grow louder and tensions between groups will begin to rise, deepening the divisions already there.

Instead of silencing what you think is obscene or wrong, try having a conversation with someone who disagrees to understand why they feel that way. You may be able not only to de-escalate the tension between groups but also to come to important compromises and conclusions through this discourse. I'm not advising abandoning your principles or ethics, I'm merely stating that a difference of opinion is no reason to resort to low-vibrational actions.

Another similarity between prohibition and the silencing of dissenting voices is the parallel economies created by each. In both cases, when you prevent someone from doing business with you, whether over the sale of liquor, a difference of opinion, or a vaccine mandate/passport, eventually an underground or parallel economy forms. This was evident in the rise of organized crime and underground bars during Prohibition. In the modern version, we're seeing people leaving jobs that require a Covid-19 vaccination and departing social media platforms for smaller alternatives that have less reach but which enable freedom of speech.

Media companies like the *Daily Wire* are putting out movies and entertainment completely outside of Hollywood's purview. People left GoFundMe for platforms like GiveSendGo when they saw that GoFundMe only gives donations to causes they agree with, as was evident regarding the Canadian trucker convoy. When you silence and ban people from participating in the public square over a difference of opinion, they are left with no choice but to form their own.

Whether both parallel economies can exist simultaneously remains to be seen. However, we do know that by forcing people to create a new public square, those in power create a toxic dynamic. People in the old public square will certainly look down on those forced to leave, creating another class of citizens and increasing the already fractured divide this country is suffering from, destroying your freedom to choose what you think is best in the process.

This phenomenon has the potential to do serious damage to the fabric of the country. This was observable in the rapid increase in crime during the Prohibition era. My biggest fear is that this will lead to a civil war completely unlike the last one. If we fought a civil war today, the divide wouldn't be based on geographical location as before; it would be based on your belief system, on ideology. This would mean that your neighbors, old friends, family, and anyone you could disagree with politically could all potentially become polarized to the point of violence. The only way to overcome this divide is to start seeing people you disagree with as humans and to have civil discussions about these disagreements in order to reach some sort of productive conclusion.

That being said, there will be times in your life when words are not enough to protect you, and you need a real physical deterrent to keep yourself safe. The best solution humans have come up with to level the playing field when we are in physical danger is the firearm. Guns, when used defensively, have been proven to save lives time and again, yet our culture today is afraid of them. The vile acts of a few bad people have convinced much of the country that guns are the problem, not the people pulling the trigger. We see them as harmful objects that kill people, rather than as defensive tools that may very well save your life.

In light of the recent shooting in Uvalde, I'll make a point to say explicitly that I am not advocating violence. Far from it. What happened in Uvalde was devastating, and was not only the result of an inept police response but also of a lack of proper measures implemented to make schools safe.

There are many ways a school can lessen the likelihood of a shooting. Having one entrance and multiple exits and armed guards such as resource officers, as well as instituting proper training from a young age on the handling and safety of firearms, are all proven ways to lessen gun violence. I'm merely stating that guns don't kill people, people kill people. We have a strange idea in America today that instead of holding a person accountable, we should hold objects responsible for the terrible acts their users have committed.

The anti-gun legislation currently enacted in several states across the country is the result of a gross mishandling of our constitutional rights. You, an American citizen, have a right to keep and bear arms that shall not be infringed. This means that "constitutional carry" is the only way your rights are not actively being infringed upon. Constitutional carry is a nickname for when a state allows concealed carrying of a handgun without requiring a permit. According to an analysis of FBI crime statistics, it was discovered that

U.S. counties that adopted constitutional carry laws such as this saw a reduction of 8.5% of murders, 5% of Rapes, 7% of Assaults, and 3% of Robberies in those counties.
(American Gun Facts, 2010)

Just owning a gun, in general, could save your life one day:

25.3 million Americans (31% of gun owners) have used a gun in self-defense. In nearly 82% of these cases, the gun was never fired.
(American Gun Facts, 2010)

This means that just brandishing a firearm to show that you're armed is enough to keep an assailant at bay, preventing a problem before it has a chance to begin. Keep in mind that many self-defense incidents are not reported to the police, so the number may very well be higher.

Constitutional carry isn't an unpopular idea either. Half of the states in the country have passed legislation to legalize it at the time of writing. The NRA's website provided a little more context:

Constitutional carry does not affect previously issued permits to carry and allows those who still wish to obtain a permit in order to carry in states recognizing existing state permits to do so. It also does not allow anyone prohibited under state or federal law from possessing a firearm to carry a firearm.

When Gov. Kemp signs this legislation, Georgia will join Alabama, Alaska, Arizona, Arkansas, Idaho, Indiana, Iowa, Kansas, Kentucky, Maine, Mississippi, Missouri, Montana, New Hampshire, North Dakota, Ohio, Oklahoma, South Dakota, Tennessee, Texas, Utah, Vermont, West Virginia, and Wyoming, in allowing law-abiding individuals to carry a concealed handgun without a government-issued permit.

(NRA-ILA and Association, 2022)

To better understand the cultural divide here, let's contrast California and New York's gun laws with Texas and Georgia's.

California:

	RIFLES & SHOTGUNS	HANDGUNS
Permit to purchase	Yes*	Yes*
Registration of firearms	Yes**	Yes**
Permit to possess registered "assault weapons"	No	No
Licensing of owner	No	No
Permit to carry	No	Yes

*As of January 1, 2015, a firearms safety certificate is generally required in order to purchase or acquire a firearm. A currently valid handgun safety certificate may still be used to purchase or acquire a handgun until it expires.

** The Department of Justice record purchases from dealers (all purchases). Residents moving into California have sixty days to register their firearms.

New York:

RIFLES & SHOTGUNS   HANDGUNS

Permit to purchase	No*	Yes
Registration of firearms	No*	Yes
Licensing of owners	No*	Yes
Permit to carry	No*	Yes

* Except in New York City.

Texas:

	RIFLES & SHOTGUNS	HANDGUNS
Permit to purchase	No	No
Registration of firearms	No	No
Licensing of owners	No	No

Permit to carry	No	No

Georgia:

RIFLES & SHOTGUNS	HANDGUNS	
Permit to purchase	No	No
Registration of firearms	No	No
Licensing of owners	No	No
Permit to carry	No	Yes

(NRA-ILA, 2014)

(Georgia is set to remove that last permit requirement for carrying a handgun by January 1, 2023.)

Looking at the contrast between two more-liberal states such as California and New York and conservative states Texas and Georgia, it's obvious to see why the cultures clash. A lot of the states that have constitutional carry have lower population densities and fewer big cities. The states that are pro-gun-control typically have higher population densities and more big cities. Constitutional-carry states understand something that the others do not: the integration of the shadow.

In Chapter One, I explained why it's important to liberate yourself from being "harmless" by integrating your shadow. The same principle applies here. States that implement constitutional carry recognize that guns can be dangerous, but instead of being afraid of them, they make it a part of their culture to educate their citizens about how to use guns more safely. This is evidence of a more integrated shadow on a cultural level, as we integrate our shadows by accepting that we can be dangerous. As before, if you don't see yourself as dangerous, you'll end up being a burden for someone who does. No one on the face of the planet is harmless, and to believe that you are any different is a lie.

The connection between constitutional carry and the shadow is important because people who are afraid of guns haven't accepted their own dangerous aspects. This is why they're afraid: they see themselves as harmless. If you give someone who sees themselves as harmless a tool for inflicting harm on others, they'll be terrified because suddenly they *do* see themselves as dangerous. The full brunt of their shadow is directly in front of them and entirely unintegrated. They're terrified because they realize the damage they can do to another person, and having never thought about that before, it stops them in their tracks.

States that have stricter gun-control laws tend to have cultures that see shadow integration as less important, and put more emphasis on group identity. The common thought in a lot of these places is "If nobody had guns, we'd all be safer. We don't need guns." The problem with this is that there will always be bad people with guns. Criminals don't typically buy guns legally to begin with. Enforcing stricter rules for gun purchases just makes it harder for law-abiding citizens to defend themselves.

Another problem with this line of thinking is that mass shootings happen for the most part in gun-free zones. According to CrimeResearch.org, 94% of mass shootings happen in gun-free zones. See the chart on the next page for a visual representation:

MASS PUBLIC SHOOTINGS IN GUN-FREE ZONES FROM 1950 THROUGH JUNE 2019

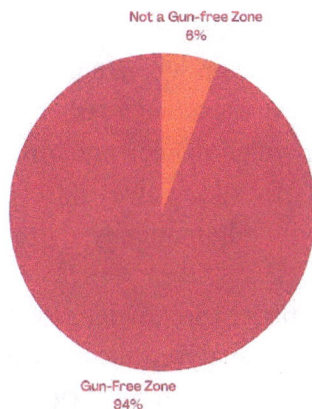

Not a Gun-free Zone
6%

Gun-Free Zone
94%

(CrimeResearch.org, 2018)

Guns act as deterrents, just like cameras do for robberies and shoplifting. When you take away the deterrent, you enable evil acts like mass shootings to occur. Guns act as equalizers. There are evil people in the world that hurt those who are more vulnerable than themselves. As unfortunate as this is, it has been a truth since the dawn of humanity that some humans enjoy hurting others.

The use of guns to prevent sexual assault is another benefit of constitutional carry. Sexual assault is a real problem, and particularly if you're a college-aged woman, a real possibility. The Department of Justice has recently released a study titled "The Sexual Victimization of College Women." The most important findings from this study show that 2.8% of college women have experienced either a completed or attempted forceful rape in just the previous seven months. Of that 2.8%, only 5% are reported to the police. Looking at that figure, the authors of the study suggested that 4.9% of college women endure a sexual assault in a given calendar year, and that perhaps 20–25% of collage women endure sexual assault during a typical undergraduate career (Woolley, 2008). This implies that almost a quarter of women who attend university are likely going to be sexually assaulted a rather bleak outlook for women. However, when women are armed with a firearm, their chances of walking away unscathed increase dramatically.

A recent paper (Southwick, Journal of Criminal Justice, 2000) analysed victim resistance to violent crimes generally, with robbery, aggravated assault, and rape considered together. Women who resisted with a gun were 2.5 times more likely to escape without injury than those who did not resist and 4 times more likely to escape uninjured than those who resisted with any means other than a gun. Similarly, their property losses in a robbery were reduced more than six-fold and almost three-fold, respectively, compared to the other categories of resistance strategy.
(Woolley, 2008)

The data clearly shows that when women carry firearms, their chances of being able to defend their lives and dignity dramatically increase. This is one of the most pivotal reasons to enact constitutional carry: an armed society is a polite society. Those who wish to do you harm are much less likely to take action if they know their lives could also be at risk. Obviously, I'm not making excuses for rapists. If someone tries to rape you, shoot them dead! Rape is one of the ultimate robberies of freedom from an individual, and if you're struggling with being sexually assaulted please reach out to the helpline below:

National Sexual Assault Hotline

Hours: Available 24 hours

1-800-656-4673

In our current political environment, your right to bodily autonomy, freedom of speech, freedom of thought and expression, freedom of association, freedom to protest, freedom of self-defense, and your right to be disagreeable are all actively under siege.

The only way forward is to come together as a country and learn to disagree peacefully again. It has long been time to bring humanity back to politics. Make a genuine, real effort to connect with people you disagree with in order to see them as friends, or at least as fellow citizens. It is time we held our government and these corporate oligarchs responsible for their negligence and direct malpractice. The only way we the people truly win is together. Freedom has never been a more important topic than it is today in the political sphere, and unless we make a serious course correction as a culture, we will be led into captivity. Embrace open dialogues. Embrace bodily autonomy. Embrace freedom.

Conclusion

It is my prayer that this book made you think. I hope you disagreed with something I said. I hope it made you think for yourself. I hope you value your freedom more than you did before and recognize the awesome power you have in your life to change. Taking everything into account, I can reasonably assert that personal responsibility, financial literacy, a connection with the spirit, a connection with God, and a radical change in one's self-perception are all vital components of living a free life.

I can just as reasonably assert that these crucial concepts of freedom have been removed from our culture, our schools, and our government. The only way that we, the American people, can overcome this systematic destruction of what it means to be free is by taking advantage of our rights while we still have them. *We must* elect better officials. We must put safeguards in place to better prevent corruption, such as by banning corporate money in campaigning, banning congressmembers from taking cushy private-sector jobs offered by big lobbyists, and by instituting term limits; there are plenty of options. It is time we as a culture and as a society took our freedoms back from the people we gave them to.

It is time to return to the spirit, to return to treating each person we interact with as a fellow human being, even if we disagree. Through the collective consciousness and our spirits, we are all connected. It is time to approach those you disdain with love in your heart instead of hate. Through the ultimate power of love, we can heal the rift. Embrace love, embrace god, embrace freedom.

Bibliography

All About Philosophy (2001) "Absolute Truth,"

AllAboutPhilosophy:

https://www.allaboutphilosophy.org/absolute-

truth.htm

Alliance for National Health (2016) "Turning Up the

Pressure on PBS – Alliance for Natural Health USA –

Protecting Natural Health," *Alliance for National*

Health https://anh-usa.org/turning-up-the-pressure-

on-pbs/

American Bible Society (1986) *The Holy Bible*. American

Bible Society.

American Gun Facts (2010) "Guns in America | Facts and

statistics about firearms in the USA", Guns in

America: https://americangunfacts.com

Anderson, J. (2018) "12 Rules for Life | Dr. Jordan Peterson |

Conversations" [YouTube video]:

https://youtu.be/Gru_JBBMBbY

Beillard, J. (2013) "Moral Relativism Is Unintelligible, ",

Philosophy Now, 97:

https://philosophynow.org/issues/97/Moral_Relativis

m_Is_Unintelligible

Belyh, A. (2017) "Why Formal Education is not

Synonymous to Success", *Cleverism*.

https://www.cleverism.com/formal-education-is-not-

synonymous-to-success/

Beres, D. (2020) "Is Christianity rooted in psychedelic

rituals?" *Big Think*: https://bigthink.com/the-

past/psychedelic-christianity/

Beschizza, R. (2021) "Adult male 'virginity' soars," *Boing Boing*: https://boingboing.net/2021/03/22/adult-male-virginity-soars.html

Brown, I. (2017) "The Irony of Tetzel's Indulgences," *There Formation Room*: https://www.thereformationroom.com/single-post/2017/03/26/the-irony-of-tetzels-indulgences

Brown, L. (2008) "Les Brown: If You Can't Be Happy, What Else Is There?" [YouTube video]: https://www.youtube.com/watch?v=MkL1lUh1X-Q

Brown, L. (2021) "'80% Dont Care & 20% Are Glad Its You!' – Les Brown" [YouTube video]: https://youtu.be/Bdgv2F0Uk9E

Byrne, R. (2016) *The Secret: The 10th anniversary edition*, Atria Books.

Cardone, G. (2011) *The 10X Rule: The only difference between success and failure*, John Wiley & Sons,

Chappelle, D. (2017) "Equanimity," *Scraps from the Loft*:

https://scrapsfromtheloft.com/comedy/dave-chappelle-equanimity-2017-full-transcript/

Crime Prevention Research Center (2018) "UPDATED: Mass Public Shootings keep occurring in Gun-Free Zones: 97.8% of attacks since 1950," *Crime Prevention Research Center*:

https://crimeresearch.org/2018/06/more-misleading-information-from-bloombergs-everytown-for-gun-safety-on-guns-analysis-of-recent-mass-shootings/

DeMatteo, M. (2020) "This is the average age when people finally pay off their student loans for good," *CNBC*:

https://www.cnbc.com/select/how-long-it-takes-to-pay-off-student-loans/

Dowling, J. (1849) *The History of Romanism, from the Earliest Ccorruptions of Christianity to the present time* Walker.

Duhigg, C. (2013) *The Power of Habit: Why we do what we do in life and business*. Lao Động - Xã .

FDA (2018) "Determining the Regulatory Status of a Food

Ingredient," *FDA*: https://www.fda.gov/food/food-

ingredients-packaging/determining-regulatory-status-

food-ingredient

FDA (2021) "Use of the Term Natural on Food Labeling,"

FDA: https://www.fda.gov/food/food-labeling-

nutrition/use-term-natural-food-

labeling#:~:text=The%20FDA%20has%20considered

%20the

Finkbeiner and Wilkinson (2018) "Divorce statistics and

facts | what affects divorce rates in the U.S.?"

Wilkinson & Finkbeiner, LLP: https://www.wf-

lawyers.com/divorce-statistics-and-facts/

Francescani, C. (2019) "What happened? Timeline of

investigation into Jussie Smollett's attack claim,"

ABC News: https://abcnews.go.com/US/timeline-

alleged-jussie-smollett-attack/story?id=61124090

Frankl, V. E. (2017) *Man's Search for Meaning*. Beacon

Press.

Gerhardt, L. (2020) "The rebellious history of the fat acceptance movement," *Center for Discovery*: https://centerfordiscovery.com/blog/fat-acceptance-movement/

Gowans, C. (2019) "Moral Relativism," *Stanford Encyclopedia of Philosophy*: https://plato.stanford.edu/entries/moral-relativism/#ForArg

Haidt, J. (2013) *The Righteous Mind: Why Good People Are Divided by Politics and Religion*, Vintage Books.

IBISWorld (2022) "Adult Obesity Rate," *IbisWorld*: https://www.ibisworld.com/us/bed/adult-obesity-rate/112885/#:~:text=Over%20the%20five%20years%20to

Jeffay, N. (2008) "Moses saw God 'because he was stoned - again.'" *The Guardian*: https://www.theguardian.com/world/2008/mar/06/religion.israelandthepalestinians

Jocko Podcast (2019) "A Good Man Is Dangerous - Jocko

Willink and Jordan Peterson," [YouTube video]:

https://youtu.be/xE0VM61O0XA

Jung, C. G. and Von Franz, M-L.. (1951). *Aion*

Untersuchungen zur Symbolgeschichte, Zürich

Rascher.

Jung, C. G., Adler, G., Jaffé, A., Hull, R. F. C. and Abbott

Pratt, J. (1973) *Letters [of] Carl Gustav Jung. Vol. 1,*

1906-1950, Princeton University Press.

Justia (2018) "Constitutional Law Privacy Rights and

Personal Autonomy," *Justia*:

https://www.justia.com/constitutional-

law/docs/privacy-rights/

Kolodny, A. (2020) "How FDA Failures Contributed to the

Opioid Crisis," *AMA Journal of Ethics*, 22(8), 743–

750.

Ladan, L. (2019) "Capitalism Remains the Best Way to

Combat Extreme Poverty," *Catalyst*:

https://catalyst.independent.org/2019/06/14/capitalis
m-remains-the-best-way-to-combat-extreme-poverty/

Lewis, T. (2020) "Johns Hopkins Scientists Give
Psychedelics the Serious Treatment," *Scientific
American*:
https://www.scientificamerican.com/article/johns-
hopkins-scientists-give-psychedelics-the-serious-
treatment/

Lukianoff, G. and Haidt, J. (2019) *Coddling of the American
Mind: How good intentions and bad ideas are setting
up a generation for... failure,* Penguin Books.

Malone, R. (n.d.) "General 2" *Robert W Malone MD*:
https://www.rwmalonemd.com/rna-vaccine-inventor

Martellozzo, E., Monaghan, A., Adler, J., Leyva, R.,
Davidson, J. and Horvath, M. (2017) "'I wasn't sure
it was normal to watch it...' A quantitative and
qualitative examination of the impact of online
pornography on the values, attitudes, beliefs and
behaviours of children and young people,"

Researchgate:

https://www.researchgate.net/project/NSPCC-OCC-pornography-report-into-UK-Children-11-16

McChesney, C., Covey, S. and Huling, J. (2016) *The 4 Disciplines of Execution: Achieving your wildly important goals*, Free Press.

Mental Health America (2022) "The state of mental health in America," *Mental Health* America:

https://www.mhanational.org/issues/state-mental-health-america

Meyers, B. (2018) "Do Hormones in the Food Supply Affect the Human Body?" S*F Gate*,

https://healthyeating.sfgate.com/hormones-food-supply-affect-human-body-2194.html

Mill, J. S. (1859) *On Liberty*. Arcturus Publishing Ltd.

Morter, S. and Taylor, J. B. (2020) *The Energy Codes: The 7-step system to awaken your spirit, heal your body, and live your best life*. Atria Books.

Muraresku, B. C. (2020) *Immortality Key: The secret history of the religion with no name*, Griffin.

Nhất Hạnh, T. and Neumann, R. (2008) *Understanding Our Mind*, Harpercollins Publishers India.

Norton, A. (2020) "Psychedelic Drug Eases Cancer Patients' Distress Long Term," *WebMD*:

https://www.webmd.com/cancer/news/20200128/psychedelic-drug-eases-cancer-patients-distress-long-term

NRA-ILA (2014) "State Gun Laws," *NRA-ILA*:

https://www.nraila.org/gun-laws/state-gun-laws

NRA-ILA and NRA (2022) "NRA Achieves Historical Milestone as 25 States Recognize Constitutional Carry," *NRA-ILA*:

https://www.nraila.org/articles/20220401/nra-achieves-historical-milestone-as-25-states-recognize-constitutional-carry

Perry, C. (2016) "The 9 Scariest Food Additives You're Eating Right Now," *Men's Journal*:

https://www.mensjournal.com/food-drink/9-scariest-food-additives-youre-eating-right-now/

Peterson, J. (2017) "Biblical Series XI: Sodom and Gomorrah" [YouTube video]: https://youtu.be/SKzpj0Ev8Xs

Pew Research Center (2016) "The roots of partisanship," *Pew Research Center*:https://www.pewresearch.org/politics/2016/06/22/2-the-roots-of-partisanship/

Pew Research Center (2017) "Partisan divides over political values widen," *Pew Research Center*: https://www.pewresearch.org/politics/2017/10/05/1-partisan-divides-over-political-values-widen/

Ross, S. (2018) "Therapeutic use of classic psychedelics to treat cancer-related psychiatric distress," *International Review of Psychiatry*, 30(4): 317–330.

Rubin, R. (2009) "Pfizer fined $2.3 billion for illegal marketing in off-label drug case," *ABC News*:

https://abcnews.go.com/Business/pfizer-fined-23-

billion-illegal-marketing-off-label/story?id=8477617

Rummel, R. J. (1990) *Lethal Politics: Soviet Genocide and

Mass Murder Since 1917*, Transaction Publishers.

Rummel, R. J. (2020) *Nazi Genocide and Mass Murder*.

Hawaii.edu:

https://www.hawaii.edu/powerkills/NAZIS.CHAP1.H

TM

Sincero, J. (2017) *You Are a Badass [How to Stop Doubting

Your Greatness and Start Living an Awesome Life]*,

Running Press.

Smith, D. J.-A. M. (2015) "What is God / Source Energy?"

Jodi-Anne's Insights into Peace and Happiness:

https://www.jodiannemsmith.com/2015/08/08/what-

is-god/

Smith, J. (1981) *Book of Mormon: Another testament of

Jesus Christ : An account written by the hand of

Mormon upon plates taken from the plates of Nephi*,

The Church Of Jesus Christ Of Latter-Day Saints.

Solzhenitsÿn, A., Whitney, T. P., Willetts, H. T., Ericson, E. E., and Peterson, J. B. (2018) *The Gulag Archipelago 1918-56 : An experiment in literary investigation.* Vintage Classics.

United States Holocaust Memorial Museum (2018) "Nuremberg Code," *United States Holocaust Memorial Museum*: https://www.ushmm.org/information/exhibitions/online-exhibitions/special-focus/doctors-trial/nuremberg-code

U.S. Department of Health and Human Services (2015) "Privacy," *U.S. Department of Health and Human Services*: https://www.hhs.gov/hipaa/for-professionals/privacy/index.html

Verghese, A. (2008) "Spirituality and mental health," *Indian Journal of Psychiatry*, 50(4): 233.

Von Bernhardi, R., Bernhardi, L. E., and Eugenín, J. (2017) "What Is Neural Plasticity?" *Advances in Experimental Medicine and Biology*, 1015: 1–15.

Woolley, R. J. (2008) "Guns Effective Defense Against Rape," *Gun Owners of America*: https://www.gunowners.org/wv26/

World Population Review (2020) "Obesity Rates By Country 2020," *World Population Review*: https://worldpopulationreview.com/country-rankings/obesity-rates-by-country

Zuber, V. (2019) "Are human rights of religious origin?" *Sur - International Journal on Human Rights*: https://sur.conectas.org/en/are-human-rights-of-religious-origin/

www.ingramcontent.com/pod-product-compliance
Lightning Source LLC
Chambersburg PA
CBHW052133270326
41930CB00012B/2860